KV-407-750

BUYING A SECONDHAND BOAT

BUYING A SECONDHAND BOAT

by Dave Gannaway

By the same author
  Boatbuilding on a Glass Fibre Hull
  Small Boat Building

First published in 1980 in Great Britain by
Nautical Publishing Company
Lymington, Hampshire SO4 9BA

in association with
George G. Harrap & Company Limited
182–184 High Holborn, London WC1V 7AX

ISBN 0 245 53446 6

Filmset and printed in Great Britain by
BAS Printers Limited, Over Wallop, Hampshire

Contents

Fig 1. 'It will never stop them from going afloat'.

1. The Matter of Choice

There are many good buys to be had in the world of secondhand boats—a market bristling with bargains for the taking. One has to search them out and the most difficult problem of all is to know a bargain when you see it. The object of this book is to throw a little light on this problem by helping you to understand the crafts of the shipwright and boatbuilder, the joiner and the painter.

High taxes and the spiraling cost of everything from a can of paint to mooring charges mean that the yachtsman has to shorten sail to bring his boating into line with his budget. Jobs that would have been done by the boatyards through the winter months now have to be done by the owner, if they are to be done at all. To some it will mean a smaller boat; to others just a lot more work. But one thing is for sure: however unfairly any Government treats yachtsmen, it will never stop them from going afloat. Fig. 1.

Traditionally the process of buying a boat was to find a craft to suit the bill, get a surveyor to give it the once over and then, if all was well, enter into negotiations with the owner over the price. The professional services of a surveyor is, as with everything else, expensive; if the craft is not up to scratch in any way then it is money down the drain, because the surveyor still has to be paid. But if the buyer is able to give the craft the once-over himself first, he can then call on the services of the surveyor when he is reasonably sure that he has found the right boat.

With a little know-how a buyer can look at half a dozen boats on his own, at little or no cost. I am not saying that within the pages of this book is enough information to by-pass the surveyor altogether. That would be ridiculous; since a good surveyor normally has a lifetime of experience to draw upon, and no amount of written knowledge can substitute experience. But if I can bring to light some of the more commonplace faults and give some idea of what to look for and where, then the reader would be well armed to do some of the preliminary footwork himself. This will save on surveying fees but not eliminate them.

Once you have found your boat and given it the once-over, then is the time to call in the professional surveyor. He will go over the boat thoroughly, and give you a written report on his findings. Only then, if he gives it a clean bill of health, should you begin to think about paying out any money. If the surveyor's report reveals any faults or items that are not as they should be, then the owner can be asked to put them right, or make an adjustment on the price to cover their repair.

But be careful! If there are faults and the owner offers to 'knock a fiver off the bill', the repair may cost you fifty. It's a cruel thing to say in this imperfect world, but it is better not to trust anyone who is selling something. Caution is the password.

What Type?   Buying a boat can be a thrill and delight; it can also be frustrating and tiresome if you are not sure what you are looking for, or even where to look. A boat is a very personal item, and, like a new pair of shoes, has to be just right if you are to get the maximum enjoyment out of it. If it is not, then your days afloat will be marred by a craft that will not do all the things you want of it.

There are many factors involved in the selection of a boat that the reader must answer for himself. Personal things like:

1 How much can you afford?
2 How many are there in your family?
3 Do you want your boat for use on the sea or rivers?
4 Is it your first boat?

Each of these questions will affect your ultimate choice. It is here that dreams and hard realities go their different ways. We have all peeled through the pages of the yachting magazines, window shopping for that dream-ship, but when we are shopping for real the choice will depend very largely upon how much money is in the kitty.

Does your wife like boats? Has she been sailing before? Many neglect this point and find their careers in yachting ruined as a result. For example, if your wife has never been sailing before and you buy a 'Flying Dutchman' and expect her to hang out on a trapeze first time out, you will scare the pants off her and kill stone dead any interest she had in boats. Be quite sure that next time you go sailing you will be looking for a crew.

In a cruising boat most women make straight for the galley, since this is their department. Many boatbuilders make a feature of their galleys since, for many a man, the main problem is to get his wife interested. Once she is happy, the battle is half over. Whoever said women are the weaker sex?

I once saw a millionaire power boat driver buy his two young daughters a small speedboat EACH, so that they could join him thrashing about the Solent. A kind gesture indeed, except for the fact that they had never been out in a boat on their own before. They were naturally very frightened, but, despite their protest, he insisted, and for the sake of peace and quiet they did, with great trepidation, cast-off. They put up a brave front for 'Daddy's sake', but I have not seen them 'come down to the boat with Daddy' since. Their interest was killed by kindness.

Another important question is that of size. How large do we need our boat, or can we afford? This can pose various other questions. How many crew will I need? Could the family manage it comfortably on their own, or would we need to Shanghai friends into crewing?

I have watched many people buy very large boats to get lots of space and accommodation, only to find that it is just too much for them to handle. They become worried about manoeuvring in rivers and marinas: the slightest puff of wind puts the whole week-end in jeopardy. Hence the boat spends the greater part of its life securely tied to its moorings, and the owner's interest in yachting quickly fades.

Fig 2. 'Not too big'.

There are people whose only desire is to go down to the boat and spend their leisure hours in the peace and solitude of the moorings, watching the comings and goings of other folk; they have no ambitions to roam the oceans but simply to get away from it all and sit quietly on the river and relax.

For many, the joy of boating is a high powered speedboat, Fig. 3. A type of craft which is most often trailed behind the family motor car. The advantages are that no permanant moorings are required since the boat is taken home after use. Trailing your boat also offers the advantage of being able to select different locations for using the boat. You are not tied to the same cruising grounds, as you are with a mooring or a marina berth.

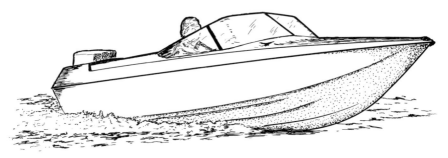

Fig 3. High powered speed boat.

A trailable boat is a good idea if you are a fisherman. Fig. 4. It enables you to select a wide variety of different fishing grounds. You can roam the coast launching your boat just where the fancy takes you. You can also use your boat on inland waterways, rivers, lakes and the like.

Fig 4. Trailable boat for a fisherman.

The serious fisherman is normally not interested in sleek shining high powered craft; he will go more often for the open launch. His requirement is a reliable, roomy, sturdy boat that will allow him to stretch his legs and give him room to move. He will often look for the refinement of a small cuddy or cabin with ample lockers for his gear. Fig. 5. He will often want to venture further out to sea in search of the

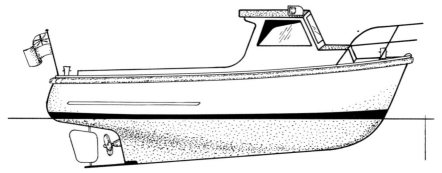

Fig 5. For the serious fisherman.

big fish; for this he will require a larger more robust motor boat to give him more protection from wind and weather.

Other trailable types of craft are small racing boats, both power Fig. 6 and sail. Many different types of boats are designed specifically for this purpose, and allow the owner to enter into competitions at venues far apart. Two of the most popular boats of this type are the Mirror dinghy and the G.P. 14, both first class craft and ideal for the purpose.

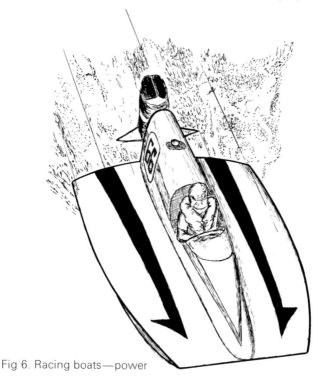

Fig 6. Racing boats—power

The range of towable craft is wide, and in general terms covers most types of craft under about 18 feet in length. Some larger craft are advertised as towable and indeed they are, but to launch, say, a 25 footer every time you want to use it is not a very practical proposition. It is very useful to be able to tow one's boat home for winter storage, but to launch it every time you want to go for a sail is out.

Cruising boats, both power and sail, require a craft large enough to sleep aboard. This does not necessarily mean a very large boat. Many ambitious cruises have been made in craft well under 20 feet in length, Fig. 7, although it must be stated quite clearly that successful open-sea passages require a high degree of skill by the skipper and that a well designed boat is not enough on its own. Yet the skills of seamanship and navigation can be learnt and the fact that you cannot navigate now should not deter you from taking up cruising.

In my opinion the first requirement to successful cruising is to have a healthy respect for the sea. I remember a famous yachtsman once saying 'you'll never beat the sea, you'd be a fool to try but if you are smart enough she'll let you win'. You can often see great ocean liners with massive steel plates ripped open like paper by the sea while a comparatively small and frail yacht can come through the same treatment unscathed simply because her master knows how to handle the situation.

But back to the boat. Recently I moored alongside a young couple in a little 16 foot sailing cruiser. We spent a happy hour exchanging chat about our various trips and I was surprised by the distance covered and the various harbours visited by them in a single short two week holiday. Two people living on such a small craft must have been a little cramped but they loved it and had a wonderful holiday, and that really is what it is all about.

Fig 8. A fine motor cruiser.

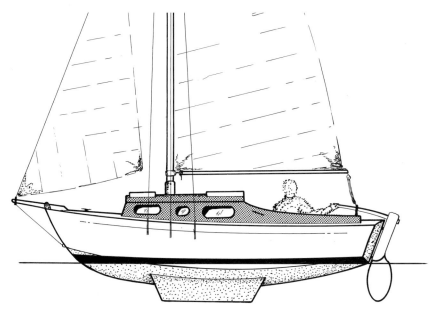

Fig 7. Small sailing cruiser. Note bilge keels.

Much the same is true about cruising in a powered craft. Fig. 8. The range of your cruise will be determined by the amount of fuel carried, and a considerable safety margin should be carried since running out of fuel at sea can be dangerous. Here the obvious springs to mind, why

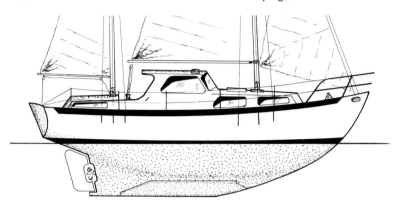

Fig 9. Motor sailer.

Fig 10. Comparative midship sections.

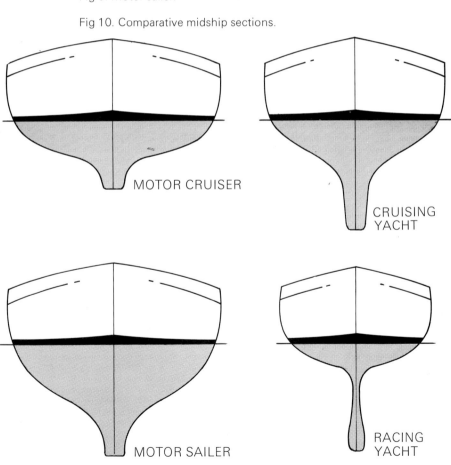

MOTOR CRUISER

CRUISING YACHT

MOTOR SAILER

RACING YACHT

not have a boat with motor and sails? Why not indeed. This is one of the most popular types of craft for cruising, the motorsailer or 50/50. Fig. 9. Why does one bother with anything else you ask? Well the answer is simply that the designer has to compromise between the fine narrow lines of a pure sailing craft and the wider bulky shapes of the displacement motor boat. The result is a boat that both sails and motors but normally the performance under sail is not quite as good as the pure sailing boat. Compare the differences. Fig. 10.

One other type of boat that often finds itself on the market is the old racing yacht converted for cruising. Fig. 11. This often produces a fine thoroughbred craft although one has to be sure the design and conversion has been done professionally; but more about conversions later.

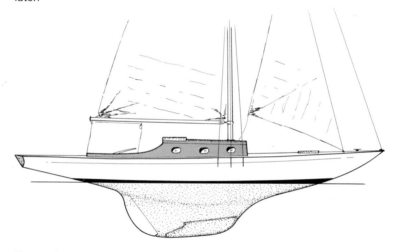

Fig 11. Older style racing yacht converted for cruising. Note no engine.

One final type of boat I must briefly mention is the power boat. The very mention of power boats produces visions of the Cowes– Torquay–Cowes type racing craft. Indeed it very often means just that. It is, after all, one of the most colourful and spectacular areas of motorboating. To see a power boat thrashing along at 60 knots has a magic of its own, that is if it is your scene. To the sailing man it often has the opposite effect. But if the growl of powerful engines and the bone shaking motion sets your blood pumping, you will no doubt know just what you are looking for in the 'For Sale' ads.

Let the growling sounds of your dream boat die down long enough for you to examine what it costs. You will no doubt already have seen attractive advertisements for power boats in the yachting press and at very reasonable prices, but here could be a stumbling block. Unlike sailing boats or motor cruisers, where once you have bought the craft the cost of running it is reasonably low, the high powered racing craft is a very very thirsty animal. I remember talking to a power boat owner

of international standing and he reluctantly gave me some of the
costing details of a racing craft.

Fuel: His boat could burn up to 60 gallons of petrol an hour. (No,
that is not a misprint.) The life of his engines, and remember they are
almost always used at full tilt, was about three races. After that the
engines had to be replaced at a price of six or seven thousand pounds
each, then there were the expensive spares and running repairs that are
always cropping up.

Even wealthy men usually find this sport excessively expensive. It is
one of the reasons why we see so many sponsored craft in the racing
fields. It is also the reason why so many appear in the 'For Sale'
columns.

It is not my intention to throw cold water on power boating and not
all craft are as expensive as the one I mentioned. It is a very exciting
and exhilarating sport that needs all the support it can get, but look
carefully at the nitty-gritty details before you buy your orange crash
helmet.

Engines

Finally a word about engines. Many marine engines are based on
successful commercial motor car or truck power units, but before they
become genuine marine engines there are various points that require
alteration in the process known as marinizing.

The most basic difference between the commercial and marine
engine is the exhaust system. The gearbox too is very different from the
type used on the road, mainly because for marine use all that is required
is one forward and one reverse gear. Unlike the engine itself, marine
gearboxes are not an offspring from the automobile; they have been
developed specifically for marine use and are available in a variety of
ratios such as 2:1 reduction, 3:1 reduction or direct drive.

Petrol, apart from being more expensive than diesel, is highly
inflammable and poses the constant risk of fire. Remember a boat may
be capable of carrying a very large volume of fuel, so extreme caution
must be exercised at all times. Petrol engined boats must be equipped
with engine room blowers to prevent any excess build-up of fumes.
They must also be well equipped with fire extinguishers.

Petrol engines are also very vulnerable to the salty damp sea air. Their
dependence upon the electrical circuitry means they must be well
looked after if any degree of reliability is to be maintained.

Unlike the petrol engine, the diesel unit is much more robust and
depends upon electrical circuitry only for starting and charging. Once
going, there is very little that can go wrong with the diesel. The
obvious exception is fuel blockage caused by dirty fuel. Most diesel
craft have fuel filters and water traps built into the system to keep this
problem to the minimum.

In general terms, if a diesel engine is going to play-up, the chances
are it will be with starting, and, although it may delay a trip or stop it
altogether, there will be no danger involved since you will still be
securely tied to your mooring.

Diesel oil is much cheaper and far less explosive than petrol, but the
unit cost of a diesel engine is very much higher.

32

Fast boats, runabouts and racing craft depend on a very high power-to-weight ratio; to get this they must use the lighter, more powerful petrol engines. On the other hand, heavier cruising boats, where weight is not a problem, most commonly use the heavier and more reliable diesel engines. There are exceptions to every rule but this is the case generally.

Finally, a cautionary note about marinizing. Since many marine engines start life as basic commercial motors, enthusiastic home engineers often decide to marinize one for themselves. A visit to the knackers yard will yield a basic truck engine for a song; but no matter how well the marinizing conversion is done, if the basic engine is not up to scratch in the first place, a dubious and unreliable unit will result. But more on this subject in Chapter 5.

Type

A very rough guide to the type of boat that would suit YOU can be determined by using Table 1. Select one item from each column and jot it down in the margin. The result will give you a good idea of what you are looking for. Make each selection carefully, taking into consideration not only what you would like, but what you can afford, what your family would enjoy, and what you could afford to maintain.

The result might be: A. 25–30. B. G.R.P. C. Power. D. Cruiser. E. Inboard Engine. F. Diesel. This reduces the almost infinite selection to a much narrower more realistic choice. We know, from the above list, that we are looking for a 25/30 foot glass fibre, diesel-powered inboard motor cruiser. That, together with the amount of money you could afford to pay for your boat, would be enough information to start a broker on the trail.

Length	Material	Use	Type	Engine	Fuel
15'/20'	Wood	Cruising	Power	Inboard	Petrol
20'/26'	G.R.P.	Racing	Sail	Outboard	Diesel
26'/30'	Ferrocement	Fishing	Motor sailer	Inboard/ outboard	
30'/up	Steel or aluminium	General purpose			

Table 1. Guide to type of boat. Note, select one from each column.

18   Buying a Secondhand Boat

Surveyors   The question of how far a surveyor should go is determined directly
by the amount of money you wish to spend. If you are prepared to pay
the earth, then the surveyor will produce a very detailed report indeed,
but generally his fee covers a good thorough check-over. His main
target is the structure, planking, timbers, decking, and beams. Very
often he will give advice to his client, such as whether the craft is good
value for money.

If there are faults in the craft, he will report them to you, and,
normally, survey their repair. As with everything else, there are good
and bad; that is some give you a better service for your money than
others. But on the whole, the standard is high and their judgement is
reliable.

There are two items on which the surveyor normally does not touch
on too deeply in the course of an ordinary survey: (a) The condition of
the ship's machinery. (b) The condition of the ship's wiring and
electrical equipment. To give a reliable mechanical report on an engine,
the surveyor would not only require the assistance of an engineer,
which adds to the expense, but also would require to try the machinery.
Both are expensive so the surveyor restricts his examination to the
exterior of the engine, the engine mounting, holding-down bolts, and
line-up.

On these matters he can draw upon his experience. He will be able to
spot tell-tale details that will help him with his judgement, e.g. drips of
oil may indicate oil leaks, perished hoses may be a sign of neglect as
will sea-cocks that have corroded solid in the open position. A very
dirty engine may have a part that is unusually clean which could lead
him to think that something is, or has been wrong. All these little
insignificant items will help him, along with his experience, to form an
accurate picture. It is all part of what you pay for when you hire a
professional surveyor.

Various engines and other items of machinery have their own
shortcomings and weaknesses. One type may be prone to shearing this
or wearing that, but it is the knowledge and experience of the surveyor
that will spot these troubles. A good surveyor can save trouble even
before it occurs.

To check the ship's wiring would involve extra expense. In a normal
survey for the purchase of the craft, if the various electrical items are all
in good working order, and the external condition appears good, it is
often assumed that the rest is satisfactory. Unlike the normal domestic
household electrical supply, which is 240 volts, the ship's 12 or 24 volt
system is much safer.

The good surveyor knows what to look for and where. By tapping
timber with a hammer he can tell its condition from the ring. (More
about that in Chapter 2.) Sometimes he can tell things by the smell. He
will often have a random through bolt taken out from a skin fitting or
P-bracket to examine it for decay. If the boat has a ballast keel, the
chances are that he will ask to have one of the large keel bolts backed
out for examination. He will tell you if any limber holes are blocked,
leaving areas of water lying in the craft unable to get away.

What the surveyor finds is not only of interest to you when buying your boat, his report may also be required when you come to get the craft insured. All in all, money invested on a survey is normally money well spent, providing the man you employ is experienced and reliable.

Just one word of warning. The surveyor's report passes comment on those parts of the craft he has inspected. I have seen reports that hedge around various items, worded like this: 'No panelling was removed but the inside planking was sound where accessible.' You see, he has simply given an opinion, he has not actually had a look. Remember that with motor cruisers and yachts most of the inside planking is covered by lockers, cupboards and linings. On the last page of the surveyor's report, you will normally find a statement like: 'This survey was completed in good faith but no responsibility can be accepted for any items whether in the report or not.' That means that the surveyor has done his best but if he has missed anything or that something was hidden from his view, he accepts no responsibility for it. In other words 'you pays your money and takes your chance'. So the more you know about it the better.

It is not my intention to knock surveyors in any way. On the whole, they are a very professional and trustworthy breed. Since you, the buyer, has to pay for his services, choose the surveyor YOU want. I always think it is best to pick a man who is completely independent and who has no ties or connection in any way with the particular craft you are asking him to survey. This way you can be sure to get an unbiased and reliable report. Indeed a good surveyor would insist on it.

Ask Around

It is very often worth the trouble of asking around. A discreet word with anyone who has been involved with the craft may well reveal good information, but take care, it can also encourage lies. Workmen involved with the craft, for instance, can often be very over enthusiastic in their opinions. This can apply equally in both directions for and against the craft. I remember an instance where one man assured me that the boat I was looking over was a good buy because 'she's been stood there, out of the water for five years, never been used'. Well any craft left that long out of the water, particularly a wooden boat, may well be neglected and have suffered as a result.

On another occasion I was told that a craft had just been re-engined. Then, after digging deeper, I discovered the reason. She had been a racing boat and had suffered structural damage as a result. So you see, a little detective work may well reveal a snippet of information that will lead to the truth about the boat's past. Of course, because a boat was used for racing it does not mean that she is in any way inferior, indeed, many are built so incredibly strongly that it is positively an asset. But so long as you know the details you can then make up your own mind.

Lloyd's

There is one word that is synonymous with surveyors and quality— Lloyd's. Lloyd's have, over many years, built up a standard and specification for the construction of a boat that is second to none. The phrase 'built to Lloyd's specification' is understood and accepted world-wide, as a sign of quality and thoroughness. Mention 'built to Lloyd's' to any yachtsman the world over and he will know that you are talking about a craft that is built to the highest order.

Lloyd's has specifications for each method of boat construction such as wood, G.R.P., steel, and ferrocement, as well as for machinery and electrical circuitry. It recommends materials to be used and those to be avoided. It lays down conditions under which specialised jobs must be carried out. An example of this is the lamination of glass fibre mouldings, where temperature, humidity and the mixing of chemicals must be carried out under carefully controlled conditions.

It is a fact that the greater part of the yachting industry bases its standards upon the recommendations of Lloyd's. Lloyd's in turn, constantly monitors new materials and methods and set down its findings. It will often offer advise and approve craft from the drawing board onward. Its surveyors are eagle eyed and very experienced and it is this which has built up its reputation.

There are various grades of Lloyd's certificates, ranging from a hull moulding certificate which covers only the moulding process, to the highest Lloyd's 100 A1. Built to Lloyd's 100 A1 is the highest possible quality using the best possible materials. It is also normally the most expensive since every operation and stage in the boat's construction is done under Lloyd's ever-critical eye. But once a craft has been issued with a Lloyd's 100 A1 certificate, you can be pretty sure that you have a well built boat.

But beware of people and companies who use the word Lloyd's to mislead you. Sadly, a good many companies, particularly the cheaper moulder of G.R.P. craft, advertise their craft as 'built with Lloyd's approved materials'. The unwary could be forgiven for thinking that a product advertised thus was of the highest order; indeed, it may well be, but the advertising blurb says 'built with Lloyd's approved MATERIALS'. This means that although Lloyd's approve the materials, they do not necessarily approve the way in which they are used, or the conditions under which they are used; nor does the resulting craft necessarily carry any warranty by Lloyd's. So be careful, many companies use this type of advertising to attract the eye and whilst they are not lying, it can be misleading.

Another point where the magic word Lloyd's can be misleading is with secondhand boats. The fact that a boat was built to a Lloyd's standard does not guarantee that it is still in that prime condition. It is one thing having a craft built 100 A1 at Lloyd's, and quite another keeping it in that same condition. A yacht built in say, 1960 to Lloyd's 100 A1, could by now, if not kept up, have all manner of defects. Remember Lloyd's is a primary insurer of boats, and to maintain its highest standards, the craft must be surveyed regularly.

Having covered the standards set down by Lloyd's, I must go on to say that there are many hundreds of other craft not built to Lloyd's that are of a comparable standard. But just as the words Rolls Royce are synonymous with the world's best motor car—so Lloyd's is to boating.

It is unfortunate that Mr Average cannot afford a Rolls Royce, so he has to buy something cheaper and that, inevitably, means being more careful in his choice. It is impossible to generalise about boats so the buyer cannot be too careful. Unlike cars, the age of a boat is not so

important. A fifty year old boat, kept in superb condition, can easily
fetch several times the money she was built for. It is also possible to
buy the right craft cheaply, renovate it and sell it at a handsome profit.
So there are no hard and fast rules about age. I have seen old fishing
boats on the Solent that were built by fishermen (unskilled
boatbuilders), and are still going strong 100–150 years later. So you see,
you really cannot tell; each craft must be valued on its own merits.

To anyone with an eye for a beautiful boat, it is often sad to see an
old craft dying a slow agonising death in some obscure creek or being
ravaged by the sea and mud. The danger is to fall in love with such a
beauty and be blinded to the hard realities of what it will cost, in time
and money, to bring her back to her former glory. Indeed, a very good
bargain can often be picked up from someone who has attempted such
a task and run out of either time, money or patience. It is possible to fall
out of love as well as into it!

Broker, Agent or Dealer

To many people, Agents, Brokers and Dealers are all the same—they
sell boats. They are in fact far from being the same. Indeed they do all
sell boats but that is where the similarity ends, and it is as well to have
an idea of the fundamental differences between them.

Broker

A yacht broker earns his living by selling your boat for you and
receiving a commission from the monies received for the sale. He never
at any stage owns the boat. He finds the customer, negotiates the deal,
and makes arrangements for finance and surveyors. He collects the
money, draws up contracts and Bills of Sale, in general seeing the deal
through. He then deducts his commission and forwards the balance to
the vendor.

His rates of commission are normally on a sliding scale, depending
upon the value of the craft. Be sure you are aware of the rates at the
outset as it is useless to start arguing about the commission rate after
the boat has been sold. Table 2 will give a rough idea of commission

Table 2. Approximate commission rates.

Selling price	Commission rate
Up to £1,000	10%
£1,000 to £5,000	8%
£5,000 to £25,000	8% on first £5,000 6% on balance
over £25,000	6%

rates, but they can vary from broker to broker, so check first. Some people prefer to negotiate a fixed brokerage fee beforehand so that everyone knows just where they stand. If your boat is a very popular and sought after type and is likely to sell easily, the broker may well be prepared to handle it for a lower figure, since he may well know where to place it or be confident it will sell quickly without too much advertising. But be sure, he will not offer this; you will have to ask, and it could save you good money.

Once you have agreed on a commission rate or fixed commission with your broker, get it down on paper, as there is no proof in telephone calls or casual chats. So to prevent any misunderstandings at the end of the deal, just ask him to confirm your agreement through the post, then you will have it all neatly written down. If he is a genuine man, he will be happy to oblige.

Check also, if your boat is on hired moorings or in a marina, whether the mooring or marina owners require a commission from the sale of your boat. Rightly or wrongly, many marinas demand a commission, normally about 1 per cent, if you sell your boat whilst it is on their premises. This is normally written into the conditions of the marina or boatyard, and it is generally displayed somewhere on the premises, usually in very small print; but it is as well to check.

Since the broker provides a service for which you pay him a commission, you, as the owner of the craft to be sold, must instruct him on the price to be asked. Most reputable brokers are very experienced on these matters, and will often advise an owner as to what a craft may be worth; but the price tag is determined by you, the owner, whether or not you take his advice. The broker's commission is taken from the money he gets for the boat, so do your sums and make sure that you price your boat to allow for his commission.

Once a broker undertakes to sell your boat he will require full details of it; these include all dimensions, type of construction, date built, name of builder, engines, speed, and fuel consumption. A full description is required of the craft's layout and, very important, an inventory of equipment and gear that is included with the craft at the asking price, e.g. dinghy, radio, etc. The more information you can supply to the broker, the better equipped he will be to sell it. One of the best aids to selling a boat is a good photograph; ask yourself what catches your eye when you are looking through the 'Boats for Sale' in the yachting magazines, of course, it is the photographs. Much brokerage business is transmitted through the post and a photograph will help to show what you have to offer.

It is also perfectly normal practice to put your boat in the hands of more than one broker. Do not make a secret of it, tell each broker who else is handling it; not only is it the straight way to go about it, it will also encourage them to get on and sell it before the other guy does. Remember if a broker does not sell he does not eat.

Agents   Broadly speaking, an agent is a manufacturer's representative. He sells the boats built by another company, and normally they are new boats. He owns the shop through which another company's goods are

Typical Brokerage Form

NAME SOLOMON		TYPE PROFILE 33	PRICE £26,500.00

LENGTH O. A.	33'0"	
LENGTH W. L.	29'6"	
BEAM	11'0"	
DRAFT	2'9"	
TONNAGE	5 ton	
DATE BUILT	1976	
FLAG	BRITISH	
CLASSIFICATION	T.S.D.Y.	
BUILDER	Profile Marine	
CONSTRUCTION	G.R.P.	
DESIGNER	Dave Gannaway	

ENGINES	MAKE	MERCEDES OM 636	DATE	1976 - 300 hours
	NUMBER	Two	SPEED	9 Knots
	H.P.	2 x 42 H.P.	CONSUMPTION	3 gal per hr max
	FUEL	DIESEL	RANGE	400 Miles

WATER CAPACITY	70 GALLS.	FUEL CAPACITY	140 GALLS.

ACCOMMODATION: For'd cabin with 6ft 2in headroom.   Carpets and fitted
curtains in all cabins.   6in zipped cushions on all berths.   Forward cabin:
two 6ft berths with stowage under, bunk cushions, lights and two shelves.
Saloon: dinette to seat 6 persons, table converts to form full 6ft 2 in
double berth, blanket stowage under, also two large drawers.   Shelves
above, wardrobes to both port and starboard.   Short settee to starboard
with drinks locker and book-case over.   Galley: S/S sink with drainer.
Full size Calor gas cooker with oven, grill and three burners.   Formica
work surfaces.   Ample cupboards, drawers and stowage.   Large fridge.
Toilet: S/S wash handbasin with h & c water.   Blake sea toilet, shower
with mixer taps, vanitory unit with stowage and mirror.   Aft cabin: two
single 6ft 2in berths, vanitory unit between with drawers, cupboards, mirror,
S/S sink and h & c water.
                    Inspection recommended.

sold. Some companies have more than one agency, some brokers are
also agents, but generally, it does not affect the purchaster in any way.
He simply goes into the store and buys the item at the price on the tag.
But since I am dealing with the buying and selling of secondhand
boats in this book, that is all we really need to know about agents.

Dealers   Anyone can be a dealer. He is simply a person or company who buys
a boat at one price and sells it for another. The dealer normally buys a
boat, paints it up or repairs it, and then puts it back onto the market at a
profit. It is as simple as that. But it is in this category that one has to
exercise the most caution.

As with car dealers, or any other type of dealer, there are good and
bad, and since a boat is such a specialised item, and as there are so
many tricky parts to it, one cannot be too careful. One of the objects of
this book is to throw a little light on to some of the things that can go
wrong, and to steer the reader clear of trouble. If you know some of the
wrinkles and tricks of the trade, you will be better equipped and more
confident to deal with it.

I have known shady dealers who discourage surveys, even advise
customers not to waste their money. Well that ought to be warning
enough since such advice must mean that the man is hiding something.
Why else would he advise against a survey? After all it is you who have
to foot the bill, not him. So don't be fooled by that sort of stunt. If he
was an honest man, he would allow you to make all the inspections
you want, even tell you of anything that was not quite right or not as it
should be.

Most well known brokers, agents and dealers, have a good
reputation and are reliable, but not all, so proceed with caution.
Unfortunately, it is not always the largest and most well known
companies who are the most reliable, and obliging. I know of a very
large company who sold a man a £15,000 yacht, and launched her into
the water for him without a single rope or fender. He had to stand and
hold onto it whilst his wife ran to the marina shop for a rope to make
her fast with. This type of thing is rare but it does happen.

As with most items of value, such as houses or cars, the purchaser, if
at all unsure, should seek professional advice before paying over any
cash; once the item has been paid for, there is very little leverage to get
anything rectified. Be sure to take the boat for a trip first since on the
bottom of your receipt will probably be the words 'as seen, tried and
tested', or words to that effect, and that means you accept the boat as it
is. So if things start to go wrong after that, it will be up to you to get
them put right. It works both ways of course, if you are selling a boat
you should never allow it to pass out of your possession until all
cheques are paid in and cleared. No matter how swell, honest or
genuine your customer may seem, clear the cheque first. Make that
your golden rule. It will not offend an honest man, indeed he will
probably respect you for sticking to sound business practice.

2. Wooden Hulls

A boat has to be hauled or lifted out of the water before any serious inspection can be made and since it is you, the prospective buyer, who wishes to have a closer look, you will also have to meet any cost involved. I have known people who have foregone having the boat hauled out and relied upon an assessment of its condition. If you have a reliable record of the craft's history this may be acceptable, but it is still a calculated risk. The only safe way is to have a good look for yourself and to do that it must come out and be scrubbed off.

Tools   Before going on to the all important examination of the wooden structure of the hull, we will first cover the tools we will need. This type of inspection is not an easy job, especially when the craft is sitting on a cold and bleak slipway in the middle of winter. Boatyards, docks and slipways are notoriously dirty places; it is surprisingly easy to step, kneel or sit in anything from a lump of grease, tallow, paint or glue, to diesel or even muddy engine oil. So the first item to secure is a pair of overalls, or, better still, a boiler suit. Since your inspection will take you right under the keel, and will often mean lying on your back in all manner of places, you will inevitably get dirty, so the more you cover yourself the better. Even if the craft has been hauled or lifted into a shep, the chances of kneeling in something gungy is just as great.

Next you will need a light to see what you are doing. Surveyors usually carry a couple of torches in their kits; most useful is the type with a square base and swiveling head, which allows the operator to set it down and focus the beam where it is wanted, leaving the hands free. Then a small torch is often invaluable for getting into small awkward places.

Best by far is an electric wandering lead, which gives an excellent light if it can be made available. It is a very good idea to include one in your kit, just in case there is somewhere to plug it in.

Spike. In the hands of an experienced operator, a spike can give a great deal of information. It must be stressed right at the outset that an owner with beautiful shiny topsides is not going to take too kindly to you if

you leave his boat peppered with a thousand spike marks. Common
sense must prevail.

The tool to use is a fine pointed spike or bradawl and the idea is to
assess the condition of the timber by ease of penetration. The skill is in
knowing how to interpret the feel of the spike. The newcomer to
surveying can best get a piece of timber identical to the structure to be
surveyed; this will set the precedent by which you can judge the older
timber of the hull. One soon becomes familiar with the different timbers
until a very accurate assessment can be made.

Hammer. Like the spike, the choice of hammers can vary greatly. A
small toffee hammer is the ideal tool. The object of the hammer is to
sound the timber, but again, before one can interpret this you must first
know the ring your hammer makes on new timber. With experience the
operator can define the clear crisp ring of sound timber from the dull
thud of suspect material.

The hammer has the advantage over the spike that it does not leave a
mark if it is used correctly. One technique is to move over the timber
with a light rhythmic tapping. This way it is easy to hear the change in
ring as you pass over soft spots. Mark the areas as you go with a
crayon or chalk. One thing to watch when using the hammer is not to
be too heavy handed or you will leave a trail of 'half-crowns' and an
irate owner; while if you hit a really ripe spot too hard, the hammer will
go in up to your knuckles.

The spike is most useful on the bottom where the little punctures will
not be evident, but the hammer is to be recommended for the topsides.

Keep recording your findings in a note book which is far more
reliable than trying to remember. Also when you come to tell the owner
he has a touch of rot in the starboard side of his hull, you can look at
your notes and state that it is, for example, twelve feet from the stem
and three planks up from the garboard. He cannot argue with that.

Worm

Beasties that eat boats. Before beginning our detailed inspection of
the hull, a word about the creatures that eat timber and keep
boatbuilders and surveyors busy. There are two or three different types
that devote their lives to making the wooden boat owner have
nightmares. The gribble is probably the most common; it is not a
woodworm as such, but a creepy-crawly with legs that it uses for
swimming, and its habit is to eat into the timber as far as it sees fit,
which can be up to two inches, then return to the surface and start
again—and again—and again. To the observant inspector, the
presence of gribble can often be quickly spotted, unlike that of the
sneaky teredo worm or ship-worm.

The habit of the teredo worm is very sneaky indeed. It starts its life a
free swimming larva, about the size of a pinhead, and then looks for a
suitable wooden home. In the case of a yacht's planking, it begins by
boring a little hole. From the shelter of that minute hole in the surface
of the timber, it quickly becomes worm-shaped and its teeth begin to
bore and eat away into the timber. Remember the only evidence left on
the surface of the timber is a hole the size of a pinhead. Incredibly, once

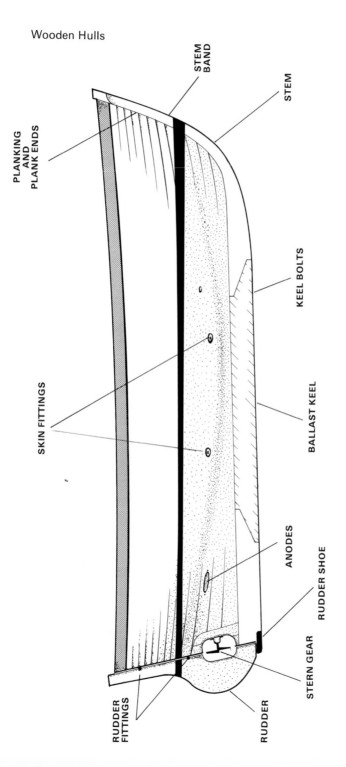

STEM BAND

STEM

PLANKING AND PLANK ENDS

KEEL BOLTS

BALLAST KEEL

SKIN FITTINGS

ANODES

RUDDER SHOE

STERN GEAR

RUDDER FITTINGS

RUDDER

Fig 12. Main areas where trouble may be spotted.

well into the timber, the teredo worm turns and continues its evil work along the grain.

In Britain, teredoes of six to nine inches have been found, while in more tropical parts of the world worms four to five FEET have been reported!

Another baddy is a little creature called martesia, which is a tropical bug with all the usual bad habits plus the added nightmare that it often attacks in enormous numbers. A thought to turn any seafarer grey.

As with any of these borers, there is very little that can be done once they arrive. The secret is to prevent them making a start and that means a thorough job of antifouling with the right product. This will also give protection from barnacles and the various other marine shrubbery that attaches itself to the bottom of the boat.

Fig. 12 shows the main areas in which trouble may be spotted, but before going into the routine of minutely inspecting the outside of the hull, stand back and have a good look at the hull as a whole. Have a look from all angles. Is the keel nice and straight? Does she have a hogged back? Fig. 13. The drawing may look like a joke but it is surprising how many vessels are affected like this to some degree. It is not so easy to spot such deformities in craft that do not have straight keels, but it can come to light by a similar unfairness along the gunwale. This type of deformity is often caused by the craft being badly supported whilst out of the water.

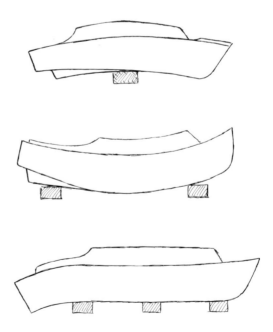

Fig 13. Possible deformities in hull shown exaggerated.

Main Structure   Stem. On older boats the stem would have been cut from a solid lump of timber, or grown crook. It was normal practice to take a template of the shape required to the timber yard or even into the woods to find a naturally shaped trunk or bow. Oak was commonly used for this and through being green or unseasoned, it often developed cracks and shakes along its grain. Often you will find these filled with putty or something similar. Fig. 14.

Solid timber stems often comprise several pieces scarphed and bolted together. Fig. 15. Check that the scarphs are still fitting nicely together and have not parted company and been filled. Filling joins of this type often has the opposite to the desired effect, since the putty or caulking opens up the gap still further.

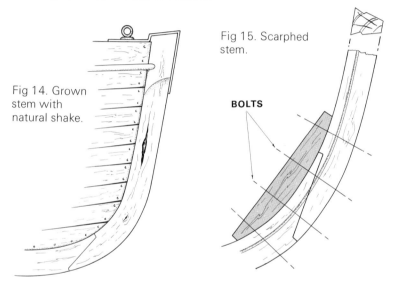

Fig 14. Grown stem with natural shake.

Fig 15. Scarphed stem.

BOLTS

Some stems are made in two pieces joining together around the rabbet line. Fig. 16. The inner part is called an apron and is bolted through the stem. The planking ends are caulked along this rabbet line

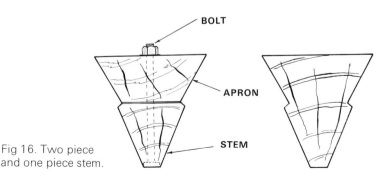

BOLT

APRON

STEM

Fig 16. Two piece and one piece stem.

and trouble is sometimes found where the caulking has been hammered in and the apron is forced away from the stem. Fig. 17. In these cases, the more caulking is hammered in the more the apron is forced away from the stem and the worse the leak gets.

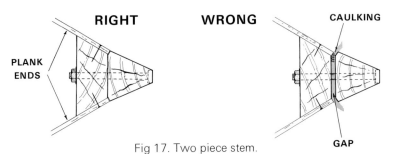

Fig 17. Two piece stem.

Modern stems may be laminated, a process developed through the introduction of modern glues; quite simply it is a series of thin strips of timber glued and cramped together around the required shape. Fig. 18. It is uncommon to find much trouble with this type of structure; almost any type of timber can be laminated but the most likely to be found in a wooden hull is mahogany or American elm.

Fig 18. Laminated stem.

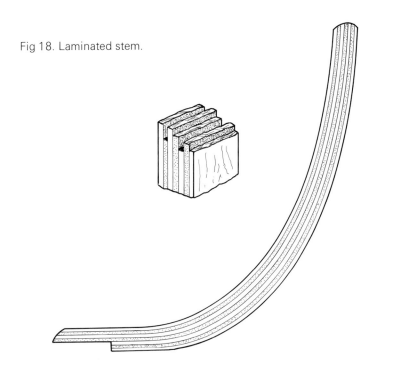

Many wooden craft are fitted with a stem band, which takes the chafe of running aground or hitting the quay wall. Often this is made of mild steel, and close examination could reveal large flakes of rust and paint falling off with very little good metal left at all. Look to see that the heads of the fixings are still in place and have not been torn off and filled. Fig. 19.

More expensive craft may be fitted with a brass stem band. These are often found to be bent or even cracked, but brass has the advantage that it can often be knocked or dressed back into shape without going to the trouble of removing it.

Take particular notice of the stem at the forefoot, which is a common spot for trouble. If a craft is beached or run aground it is often the forefoot that takes the crunch first; it is also this same spot that takes all the chafe if the rubbing band is not fitted or is missing. It is common enough to find one or two 'little shipwrights' or pieces let-in in this area. But if it is likely to receive excessive wear through constant beaching then an effective rubbing band or metal fashioning piece should be fitted. Fig. 20.

If the craft you are inspecting is already fitted with this type of fashioning piece, try to determine if it was fitted for that purpose and not to cover damaged plank ends or rot.

Once the hull has dried off after being hauled out of the water, the

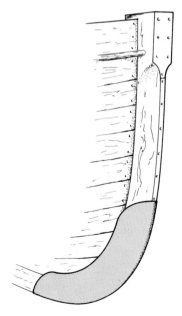

Fig 19. Metal chafing piece or shoe.

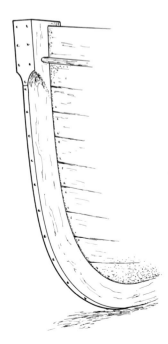

Fig 20. Metal stem band.

tell-tale signs of wet strips along some of the seams of the planking may also be a pointer to trouble. Common enough in older wooden craft, it quite simply indicates that water within the hull is seeping out. There can be various reasons for this but more commonly it is quite simply faulty caulking and can be cured by raking the old saturated boat cotton or oakum out and replacing it in the traditional way.

Look out for other areas where water may be leaking OUT of the hull. Most often this type of leak will be confined to the area along the keel because that is just where any water left in the boat would lay. I have known craft leak out water for several days after being hauled out of the water. Just one cautionary word on this point is that it is a complete waste of time and money trying to eradicate a leaky bolt whilst everything around it is still wet. Everything must be thoroughly dry before a successful repair can be made.

Treat any tingles or patches with suspicion as they are obviously there to cover some sort of trouble. Fig. 21. Take more trouble over your inspection when the tingles get excessively large which could mean big trouble.

Fig 21. Copper patches and tingles.

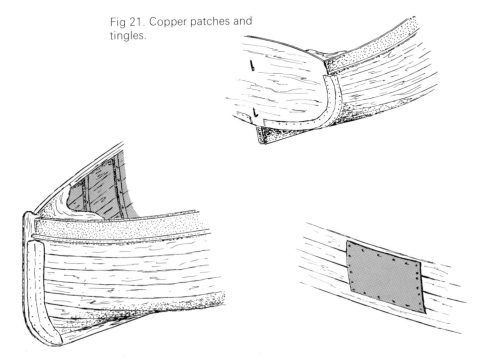

Look out for glass fibre patches on a wooden boat. This is bad practice since G.R.P. and wood, particularly wet or damp wood, do not always provide a good permanent bond to each other.

Wooden hulls that have been completely sheathed with glass fibre should also provide you with a large question mark. There are very mixed feelings about the effectiveness of G.R.P. sheathing of old wooden craft. In my experience, for every successful job, there is a string of failures; old boats tend to move, they work and if the G.R.P. sheathing is rigid then something has to give; once the bond between the hull and the G.R.P. has gone there is a gap to fill with water and trouble, because the water will lay between the two, unable to get out.

I know of a case where an old 50 foot motor yacht had her complete bottom sheathed with G.R.P. On her very first outing after the job had been completed, a huge section half the length of the boat came away from the hull, dragging much of the old caulking out as it did so with near disastrous results. There was nothing wrong with the glass but the old hull was cranky and flexed more than the G.R.P. would allow; together with the water pressure caused by the screws, the bond was just not good enough and away it came.

Before going on to describing what troubles to look for in the planking of a wooden craft, we will look briefly at the various types of planking likely to be encountered.

Planking

Carvel. Of the five different types mentioned here, the most common is carvel planking, Fig. 22, where planks are shaped and fitted edge to edge around moulds and secured to bent timbers or grown frames. The outside edges are bevelled to form a seam which is caulked or splined, with caulking being the most common. Craft with splined seams were normally special craft, such as expensive racing yachts and yachts' tenders.

Clinker. Fig. 23. Traditionally one of the quickest methods of planking, each plank is shaped and fitted to overlap the previous one. Generally, clinker planking is restricted to smaller craft such as ships' lifeboats, launches and dinghies. A clinker boat, as a carvel one, is built around a set of moulds and timbered when all the planks are fitted. Fixings are normally copper nails, clenched on the inside; this type of fixing is most suitable because the nail is drawn up very tight as it is clenched or riveted. Other methods of fixing are described on page 35.

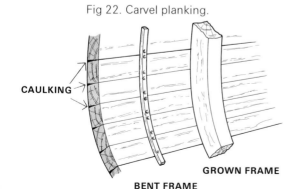

Fig 22. Carvel planking.   Fig 23. Clinker.

CAULKING

GROWN FRAME

BENT FRAME

Double diagonal. Fig. 24. This method is most often encountered on
military and such like craft. Two layers of planking are laid at right
angles to each other over ridged frames. Normally, between the two
skins is a layer of calico covered with linseed oil. One drawback with
this type of construction is the difficulty in repair.

Seam battens. Fig. 25. Like double diagonal the seam batten method is
most often found on craft built for the armed forces, and normally of
the chine type of construction. Each plank edge or seam is joined on a
batten, hence the name.

Plywood. Fig. 26. Probably the most modern of the methods described
and likely to be encountered, it is restricted to craft of the single or
double chine type. There are various dinghies that have been clinker
planked in plywood, but generally speaking, these are exceptions rather
than the rule.

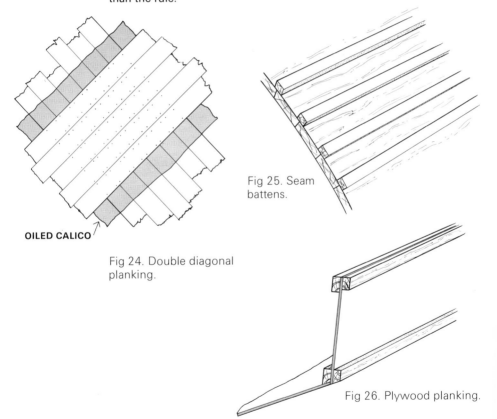

OILED CALICO

Fig 24. Double diagonal
planking.

Fig 25. Seam
battens.

Fig 26. Plywood planking.

Fixings   Many fastenings may be found in various forms of hull structures,
ranging from the most traditional of all, the trun'le or tree nail, which is
a round dowl of timber, to the most modern spiked or gripfast nail. Let
us look at some of them. Fig. 27.

Copper nail and rove. This is probably the most common fixing in a wooden hull. It is a square copper nail with a rove that is forced tight upon it and clenched or riveted up.

Turned copper nail. This is similar but instead of using a copper rove, the end of the nail is turned back into the timber.

Galvanized nail. Boats built on the Continent of Europe sometimes have the planking fixed with galvanized nails. This is a good fixing since the roughness of the galvanizing holds in the timber rather like a barbed nail.

Dumps. Commonly found in very heavily built craft of the motor fishing vessel type, the dump is a large square nail with a chisel point and countersunk or raised head. Most often it is galvanized, although it may be plain mild steel. They are sometimes referred to as spikes.

Clout nails. These are similar but round instead of square and they too have a chisel point.

Gripfast nails. These are barbed nails normally of bronze and give excellent holding power.

Wood screws. These are sometimes used in planking where the timber is too thin to receive a nail.

Copper tack. Used for securing calico between the planks of double diagonal structures and elsewhere where a small nail is required.

Coach screws. Found mainly on heavy hull structures, used to fix floors, iron knees, or heavy deadwoods.

Bolts. Bolts are normally used where an internal floor is secured through the planking. The material of the bolt has to be compatible with the materials it is securing, such as mild steel, galvanized or brass.

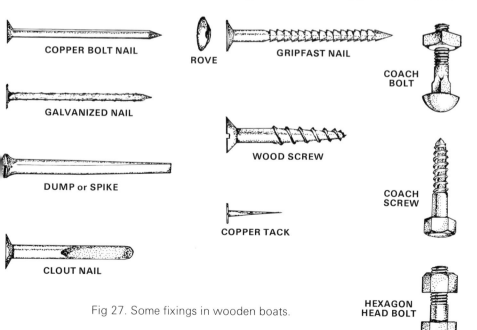

Fig 27. Some fixings in wooden boats.

Age   The age of a craft and the condition of its timber have nothing
whatever in common. Unlike a motor car which, generally speaking,
begins to decay and devalue from the moment you buy it, an old boat
can very easily be in near perfect condition 20 years after it was built;
even more important, it can be worth many times the price for which it
was built. There are many theories as to why so many old boats last so
long but I feel sure it is nothing more magical than the fact that the
timber used was of prime quality, perfectly seasoned and expertly
selected.

Looking for trouble in the planking is not so easy when a hull is fully
painted. If we could have all the paintwork burnt off back to the bare
wood, the task would be a simple one, but alas, it seldom is. But since
most trouble such as rot starts on the edges of timber, that is where we
must concentrate our attentions.

Plank ends are where faults can often be found. Split ends, caused
by driving extra nails into a plank end without first drilling a pilot hole
is common enough. Fig. 28. Fitting very short ends of planking is not a
good practice and is the mark of an amateur. Fig. 29. This must not be
confused with a stealer which is fitted at the time of building. Fig. 30.

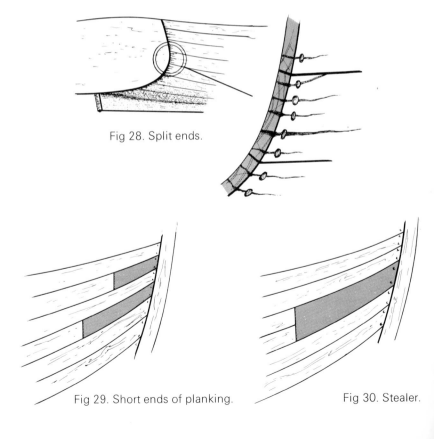

Fig 28. Split ends.

Fig 29. Short ends of planking.   Fig 30. Stealer.

A short end of planking means one of two things: (A) a damage repair or (B) the removal of rot. In older craft this type of repair becomes more evident because a different type of timber may have been used. The hull originally may have been planked in oak, larch or pitch pine, timbers which are not common now so the chances are that the repair would have been done in a more readily available timber, such as mahogany. Later, when you inspect inside the craft, remember to check that the ends of the short ends of planking are fitted with butt straps: but more about that later.

The plank end fitting may change as the planking reaches the lower part of the stem. Fig. 31. This is good practice and quite normal.

Where very wide planks are used, a bowing in the planks may be found. Fig. 32. Splitting may be found where an attempt has been made to fit it back by knocking a nail through its centre.

Water seeping from the seam in the garboard strake can indicate faulty caulking or slack fastenings. All old caulking and stopping must be removed by raking out before the plank can be refixed.

Rust marks running down the ship's side are indications that the galvanizing on a bolt has broken down. These are normally easy to find.

If areas of soft planking are found, then you should work outwards with the spike or hammer to determine just how far the trouble extends. Then go just a bit more to make sure you have covered it. To repair damage or rot in carvel planking is straightforward enough by removing the affected length and replacing it. With clinker planking the same is true but great care is needed not to damage the adjoining planks on either side. Double diagonal is by far the most involved type of planking to repair since to make good a small area of damage or rot, a very large area of planking should be removed. Where this has not been done, and a repair job has been skimped, perhaps with a badly fitted patch, then trouble can be expected.

Many boats of double diagonal build have very large chine rubbers to cover the edges of the planking. Fig. 33. It is common practice and a

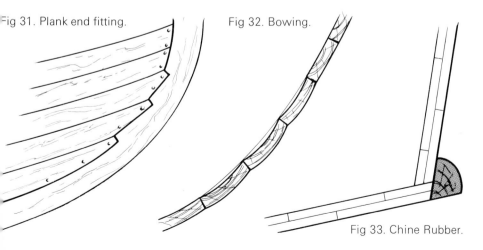

Fig 31. Plank end fitting.   Fig 32. Bowing.

Fig 33. Chine Rubber.

very bad one, for some boatyards to shore-up the boat under these chine rubbers which drives them out of shape. Fig. 34. The result is that they become loose and fail to provide the protection to the plank-ends that they should.

Fig 34. Shoring-up a chine boat.

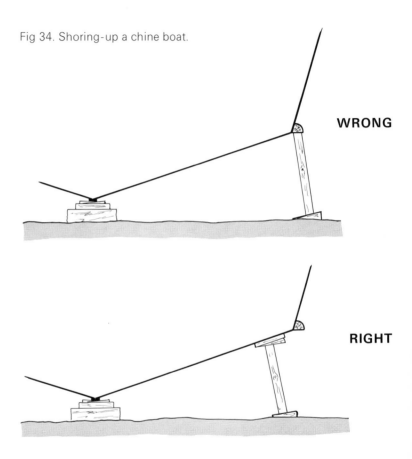

WRONG

RIGHT

Fittings   Rudders. If the craft has an external rudder, Fig. 35, check the gudgeons and pintles for wear. Give the fitting and rudder a good yank in all directions to see if there is any movement. It is quite common to find securing bolts badly corroded and slack in the holes, or even missing altogether. If the rudder has a shoe on its heel, check that closely too, as wear is often found where the rudder stock sits into the shoe. This is most often caused quite simply by years of use where the rudder has moved constantly back and forward, aided by the grinding action of grit and sand; a bearing of some sort is often found here.

With a spade type rudder, Fig. 36, check the play in the bearings,
again by wiggling the rudder blade. Don't expect them to be an
engineering fit, but then not too slack either. If the rudder is made of
metal, it may well have its own anode, but check for corrosion anyway.

Fig 35. Rudder fittings.

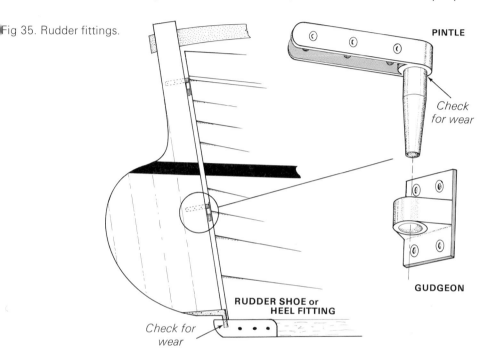

PINTLE

Check for wear

GUDGEON

**RUDDER SHOE or
HEEL FITTING**

Check for wear

Fig 36. Bearings with a spade type rudder.

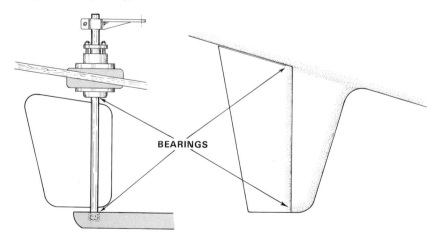

BEARINGS

Propellers. There are various ailments that propellers can suffer from, but in general, they can be reduced to two main groups; (A) Physical damage, e.g. knocks and chips caused by hitting obstructions. (B) Corrosion, e.g. electrolytic action, cavitation burns.

Damage to the (A) group is relatively simple to overcome, the propeller has simply to be removed and repaired. Group (B) is by far the biggest problem, as the cause of the trouble is not usually obvious.

Fig 37. Checking propeller bearing for wear.

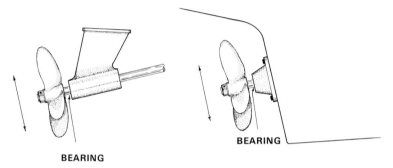

BEARING

BEARING

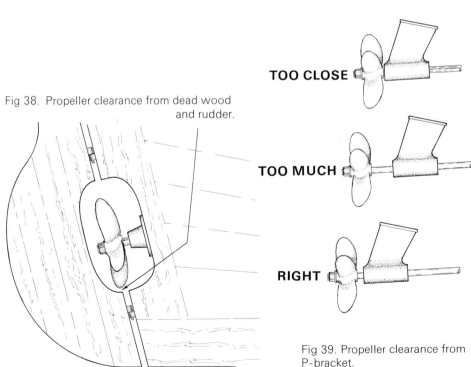

TOO CLOSE

Fig 38. Propeller clearance from dead wood and rudder.

TOO MUCH

RIGHT

Fig 39. Propeller clearance from P-bracket.

Check that the nut holding the propeller onto the shaft has a split pin through it. I have known boatyards fit mild steel split pins through stainless steel nuts, with the result that after a short time afloat, the split pin vanishes.

Take hold of the propeller, just as we did for the rudder and try to move it from side to side. This will check crudely if there is any wear in the propeller shaft's bearings. Fig. 37. Where a P-bracket is fitted, the bearing is normally a rubber cutlass type and, if worn, can be changed by sliding out the old affected unit and replacing it; it is normally retained by a small grub screw in the side of the P-bracket. Excessive wear to propeller shaft bearings can be caused by a propeller that is damaged or out of balance. Once out of balance, it will cause vibrations, excessive wear, and also discomfort.

Whilst in this area, we can check to see that the propeller has enough clearance from the hull. Table 3 gives a table of clearances for the various sizes of propellers, ranging from six inches to eighteen inches. Where a propeller is fitted in the cut-out of a skeg or deadwood, Fig. 38, the clearance would apply at both top and bottom. And whilst talking about clearances, check the gap between the P-bracket or stern log and the propeller, Fig. 39. This should be approximately one inch. For a 12 in. to 14 in. propeller, the clearance given in Table 3 will also provide a useful guide. If you require to know the size and pitch of the propeller, by cleaning off the area between the propeller blades you will usually find the two dimensions stamped into the metal.

Table 3. Hull clearances, for various propeller sizes.

Diameter of propeller	Minimum clearance
6" (15.25 cm)	$\frac{1}{2}$" (1.25 cm)
9" (22.75 cm)	$\frac{3}{4}$" (2.00 cm)
12" (30.50 cm)	1" (2.50 cm)
15" (38.00 cm)	$1\frac{1}{4}$" (3.25 cm)
18" (45.75 cm)	$1\frac{1}{2}$" (3.75 cm)

**Propeller
Brackets**   In wooden craft, there are two main types of propeller brackets,
             Fig. 40:
             (A) P-bracket,
             (B) A-bracket.
             Many of the older type A-brackets were incorporating a skeg. Both
             of these types of brackets most often have a hardwood pad fitted
             between their palm and the hull, if cracked or damaged this can be
             another cause of leaks.

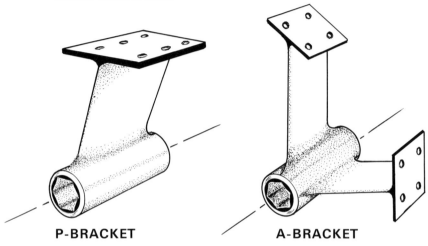

P-BRACKET   A-BRACKET

Fig 40. Types of propeller bracket.

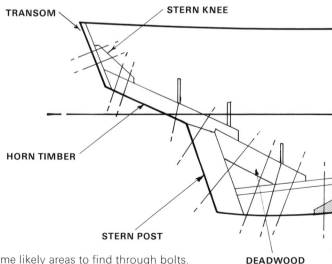

Fig 41. Some likely areas to find through bolts.

P-brackets. Examine the P-brackets, in particular the holding down bolts. If the heads are covered with years of grime and coats of antifouling, the chances are that they will be in order. If you spot a hairline crack around the head of the bolt, it could mean that the bolt is slack and needs tightening up, or it could indicate some form of cathodic action; whatever it is, have the bolt removed for examination. I have seen several examples where both the head of a bolt and the nut on the other end have been in good condition, yet two inches of bolt in between have been missing. It is not a bad idea to give the bolts a good tap with a hammer. This could result in a clear healthy ring from a good fixing, or it may surprise you as the end of the bolt falls off.

Skin fittings. It is usually a good idea to back out at least one of the bolts to the toilet sea cock skin fitting, then examine it closely for any tell-tale signs of decay. Discolouration of the metal or even the presence of minute deposits of salts can give the clue that trouble is afoot. There are companies that specialise in X-ray examinations, although that service would be extra to a normal survey.

It's an idea to select various bolts at random and have them removed for inspection. An indication of other areas where through bolts are to be found is shown in Fig. 41.

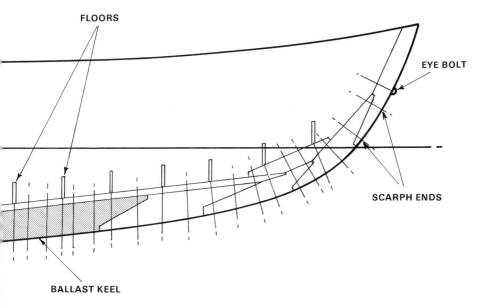

FLOORS

EYE BOLT

SCARPH ENDS

BALLAST KEEL

Cathodic
Protection

To delve into the theories of corrosive troubles and their causes is a subject best suited to the expert. I am broaching it simply because it is an important and often neglected item. My descriptions here are unashamedly simple; for the reader who wishes to delve deeper I recommend they contact people such as Peter Tier of M. G. Duff and Partners Ltd, who have made extensive studies of these problems.

Have a good look at the anodes, a great deal can be learned by their condition. If the boat has been in the water any length of time, there should be signs of decay evident on them. Lack of any erosion can mean as much trouble as excessive decay. It could indicate that some other metal item on the craft's underwater area has become anodic and hence is being, or has been, decayed. Lack of decay can also mean that the anodes have not been wired-up correctly inside the boat, or they have just been put on new.

At the other end of the scale, the anodes may have gone completely. This can also spell trouble since once the zinc has gone the electrolytic action will then turn to the next metal in the galvanic series. This could be a fastening or bolt somewhere, hidden from view, or a P-bracket bolt, keel bolt or rudder fixing. There is no telling where the action will start next. But be sure that every boat which lives in the sea is fitted with some form of cathodic protection.

Sacrificial anodes are normally made of zinc, which must be of special high purity and not simply cast from any zinc material conveniently available. They can be purchased as a standard chandlery item.

A check should be made to see that the anodes are in fact wired-up to all the items that require protection. Fig. 42. Toilet skin fittings and keel bolts may also be wired in. If the engine has a flexible coupling

Fig 42. Wiring the anode.

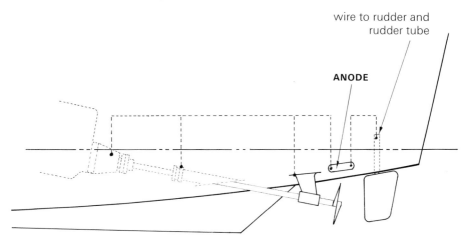

wire to rudder and
rudder tube

ANODE

check that it has a wire bridging one side of the coupling with the other. Fig. 43. As flexible couplings can insulate propeller shafts and propellers form the main cathodic protection system the shaft is sometimes fitted with an anode of its own.

Galvanic corrosion is always there; it continues day in and day out, 24 hours a day. If that is not enough, galvanic corrosion can occur within a metal, that is a metal item can be affected by galvanic corrosion on the inside whilst giving no clue of it on the surface.

Electrolytic corrosion is another nasty that can be caused by leakage of current from the craft's electrical system. The only real cure for this is to totally isolate the batteries at a suitable master switch before leaving the boat unattended for some time. So check that a master switch is fitted. Faults with installations such as reversed polarity can cause rapid loss of metal. Another bad practice is to use skin fittings for earthing high output radios and the like.

A craft with twin engine installations should have two anodes wired independently; steel rudders and bilge keels often have an anode attached directly to them. Fig. 44.

Fig 43. Wire to bridge sides of coupling.

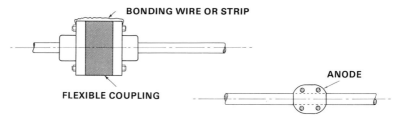

Fig 44. Steel rudders and bilge keels often have anodes attached.

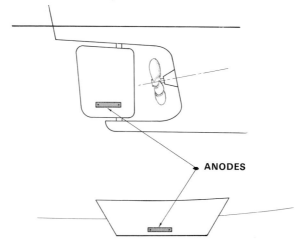

Modern boats with inboard/outboard engine units normally have their own cathodic protection system built into the propeller unit; these are normally in the form of a zinc ring fitted directly behind the propeller and a zinc block attached to the underside of the housing to maintain cathodic protection even when the propeller unit is in the raised position. They can be checked by removing the propeller.

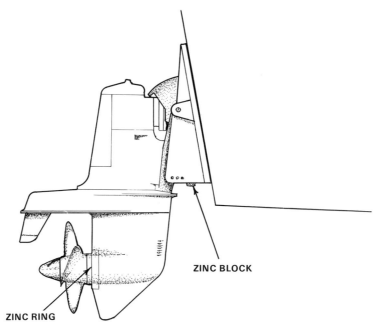

ZINC BLOCK

ZINC RING

Fig 45. Typical cathodic protection to inboard/outboard engine.

Note that timber can be affected by an electro-chemical process causing decay or rot. It is the result of electro-chemical effects of metal passing through damp timber causing an alkaline condition which in turn will cause a breakdown in the timber; the degree of breakdown depends upon the variety and type of timber. For example, pitch pine and teak are very resistant to this form of breakdown, but mahogany is very susceptible. The alkaline solution breaks down the nature of the timber to cause softening and cracking when the timber dries.

Table 4 lists the galvanic series, but it must be pointed out that some metals, including aluminium and stainless steel could be placed in more than one position in the scale, since there are so many different types. The differences depend upon their chemical make-up and other factors since when looking at the metal it is impossible to be certain.

For practical purposes, it can be said that the closer the metals in the galvanic series are together, the less will be the corrosive effect.

How long will anodes last? Provided the recommended types and sizes of anodes have been fitted, they should last for at least a full

Table 4. Galvanic Series.

ANODIC—ACTIVE
Magnesium Alloys
Zinc
Galvanized Mild Steel
Aluminium Alloys
High Tensile Steel
Mild Steel
Wrought Iron
Stainless Steel—Active
Lead
Gunmetal
Manganese Bronze
Naval Brass
Yellow Brass
Aluminium Bronze
Silicon Bronze
Copper
Monel
Stainless Steel—Passive

CATHODIC—NOBLE

season with ample margin of metal in hand. Actual rate of corrosion can vary widely, however, under different conditions. Anodes remain fully effective until they have been reduced to 20 per cent of their original size, when they should be replaced. Small boat owners normally replace anodes once a year when their craft are lain-up for fitting-out.

As I stated at the beginning of this chapter, I intend to touch only very lightly on this very involved subject but the reader who wishes to delve deeper into the mysteries of corrosion, galvanic or electrolytic, should contact one of the specialists on the subject stating their individual problems.

3. G.R.P. Boats

Glass fibre production is used for the vast majority of new boats today, ranging in size from a child's model to a fully fledged naval minesweeper. Every conceivable type, shape or form is available in glass fibre, a material that is ideally suited to boatbuilding since it can be easily formed around the strangest shapes with ease. In fact the more shapes that are formed in G.R.P. the stronger the structure becomes, rather like the strength achieved by corrugating thin tin. The result is a structure that is both light and very strong.

Boatbuilders who built previously only in wood were forced by common demand to learn the strange new techniques. Traditional boatbuilders with little or no chemical knowledge, dropped 'clangers' as they learned the G.R.P. process, and experts in G.R.P. laminating did the same whilst they learned about boats. Everyone was learning. The results were that a good many of the early glass fibre craft were not all that they should have been.

It would be quite unfair to say that all elderly G.R.P. boats are suspect, far from it; many are still giving excellent service, and some of them are working craft with an impressive record. I am merely warning that a considerable amount of questionable boats were built, particularly small craft, and many of them must still be available.

Another questionable area was that of design. Craft that were successful whilst traditionally built in timber turned out to be lacking when produced in glass; this was common with dinghies and small boats. I recall a company moulding a clinker dinghy in G.R.P. and, unlike its wooden original, the result was an almost certain ducking for anyone who dared to step in it. There are still many hundreds of those dinghies around today.

Whilst all this is inevitable in the course of development it does leave the products of these experiments to pop up on the open market as another trap into which the unsuspecting could fall.

Modern craft, on the other hand, are now produced to a very high standard indeed. A vast amount of knowledge learned about these strange and complex materials now virtually eliminates most of the problems; standards have been set and rules produced to ensure that boats are built to get the most out of the remarkable qualities of this material.

Lloyd's has produced a set of rules which is very comprehensive indeed. It covers details such as the required percentage of catalyst to resin or the conditions under which the laminating must be done. More of that later. But there are no laws to stop the fly-by-nights from setting up in business to produce cheap junk. There are, sadly, such companies still around.

When buying a secondhand boat the majority of faults in G.R.P. fall into three categories:

(a) Cosmetic repairs; chips, tarnishing, minor scratches and abrasions.
(b) Minor repairs; small holes, blisters and star cracks.
(c) Structural repairs; large holes, areas where the glass is missing and require reforming.

Cosmetic Repairs

Most secondhand craft will have received some minor damage, scratches and scuffs during normal use. Chips in the gel coat can be expected in a well used boat; there is the exception where a skipper is ultra cautious and goes to great lengths to maintain perfection in his boat, but normally there is a series of blemishes about the craft that need a 'good-coat-of-looking-at'.

Chips, scratches and deep scores are all easy to repair, since they affect only the outer gel coat surface. The biggest problem here is to match-up the colours perfectly. Even on a white surface the chances are that the white of the repair will show if you look closely. It all depends upon how close a colour match you will settle for. If nothing but perfection will do, and there are a lot of repairs, then you will probably need to paint the whole area in a two-pack polyurethane paint.

I was recently involved with a large new yacht that had a streaky gel coat finish on the hull. The polyurethane paint manufacturers made a perfect colour match for the job and the whole job was coated up. Following the instructions to the letter with regard to temperature and conditions left the hull with a finish that was every bit as good as the original gel coat. Technically these two-pack paints are actually harder than the gel so should last for a considerable time. If there is any drawback then it will be in the areas where chafe occurs. Paint, even though it is harder, does not have the thickness of gel so is vulnerable to excessive wear.

I am sure it is a process that is here to stay; already a number of yacht and boat manufacturers are producing new craft finished in this way and more and more owners of secondhand boats are giving them a new lease of life with a lick of two-pack-poly. But it is very important to follow the makers' instructions particularly with regard to the temperature required. I have seen boats painted in very cold boat sheds with the result that the paint took so long to dry that it had collected a layer of dirt and muck. The resulting craft looking worse after painting that it did before.

The most common blemishes that can spoil the beautiful finish of a G.R.P. boat are small scratches; these can vary from a deep score to a smudge of micro scratches. They are easy to repair using a matching coloured gel.

The reason such scratches are so annoying is that they fill with dirt and become even more conspicuous. A mass of scratches, say where the dinghy has been rubbing alongside, will almost vanish after a wipe-over with a cleaner. Another treatment is to burnish with a cutting back compound like 'G7', 'T' cut or even·Brasso.

Star Cracks

Star cracking is another very common fault often encountered in secondhand G.R.P. craft especially in areas of high stress, such as around the base of stanchion feet or cleats. It is often caused by impact or in an area that is insufficiently reinforced.

Another factor that can help to cause this condition is a gel coat that is too thick. Gel on its own is brittle and if too thick will star easily; the gel coat layer should not be thicker than 0.6 mm. The pattern of the star cracking will very often give a clue to its cause. Fig. 46A shows that the area to which the stanchion is fixed is not rigid or reinforced enough. This effect can often be encountered around cleats, bollards, handrails and chainplates, where high concentrated stresses occur.

Fig. 46B is another common condition. A pattern of horizontal cracks may appear where a coachroof, wheelhouse or upstanding hatch is not sufficiently strengthened at the base. Fig. 47. Some surveyors refer to this as the hinge effect; it is sometimes also found in cockpit mouldings and internal mouldings. Fig. 48 illustrates some of the areas where this problem is most often found.

Figure 46C is a type of star crack every bit as common as the rest; it is caused by a single impact, which can originate from outside or in.

Star cracks that are caused from an external source, such as hitting the quay wall or dropping something very heavy onto the deck, are not

Fig 46. Star cracks.

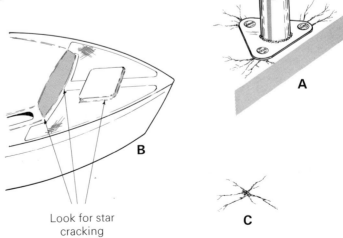

Look for star cracking

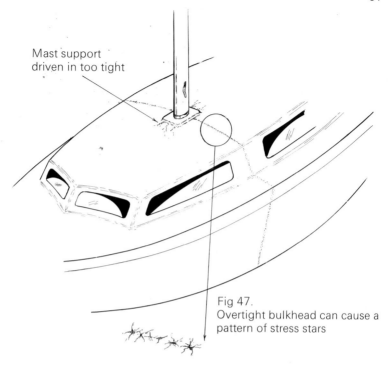

Mast support
driven in too tight

Fig 47.
Overtight bulkhead can cause a
pattern of stress stars

too much of a problem. They can be repaired and the surface brought
back to original, and that is that. Cracks caused from within the boat
are more of a problem. A bulkhead that has been fitted too tightly or a
mast support that has been driven into place by an over zealous

Fig. 48 Hinge effect.

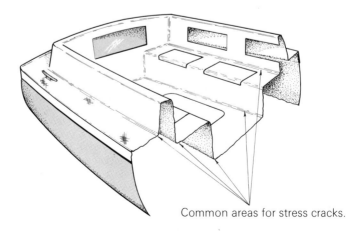

Common areas for stress cracks.

boatbuilder are but two causes. Extreme conditions of this may result in a whole series of star cracks forming along the line of stress.

Whilst talking about star cracking, I will just mention one little incident I spotted some time ago. The problem was a series of star cracks in a new boat that had never been in the water. The irate owner insisted that the cracks were the fault of the boatbuilders, but after very close inspection it was discovered that the star cracks in question were in fact in the original mould and that they had been faithfully reproduced on every hull. They were in truth not cracks in the gel but lumps, fine little ridges which were easily removed with wet and dry. This is not uncommon since many G.R.P. laminators use a little too much brute force to remove products from their moulds. It is a very bad practice to hit a mould direct, and most laminators keep a rubber hammer to hand as a persuader should it be needed, but even that can produce some nasty wounds on a G.R.P. mould.

Humps and Bumps

Due to the high cost of constructing plugs and moulds for glass fibre boats, the manufacturers normally make quite sure that the resulting item is of high standard. It is, in fact, quite unusual to get mouldings with any humps and bumps in the outer surface. This being true, if you are looking over a boat that does have any irregular humps or bumps, be suspicious and ask yourself why.

The most common reason for this type of effect is quite simply that the craft has already been repaired and that the repair is defective or was not done correctly in the first place. If a little prodding with a bradawl reveals traces of filler, it could mean that the area has been more botched-up than repaired. I am not saying that the use of filler is a sign of a bad job, but the use of too much filler does not make for a good repair.

I have seen many boats that have been so-called repaired, using mountains of filler. The result may look like a perfect job when first complete, but after a little time in use the filler, being rigid, will soon show itself by cracking as the more flexible G.R.P. moves all around it. It is not quite the miracle material many imagine it to be. How many motor cars have you seen where great lumps of filler have fallen off where repairs have been made? The reason is the same, the steel of the car is flexible and rusty and the filler is hard and as rigid as rock. With a car, the filler will probably fall off and take the rusty part with it. On a G.R.P. surface of a boat, it should not fall off because it should be chemically bonded but that will not stop it cracking.

If the same repairs had been done using resin and matt in the orthodox way, surfaced with filler, the repair would be undetectable and permanent. The reason it is seldom done in this way is simply that it takes a little more time and trouble. In fact it can be said about a repair, 'If you can see it, it is not right'.

Much the same can be said for hollows as for bumps. One cause of hollows is a heavy impact which has caused a tear in the G.R.P. making the surface no longer flush. Fig. 49. Where the operator has not bothered to cut back the defective area to retain the correct form, a bad hollow will result.

Fig 45. Structural repairs.

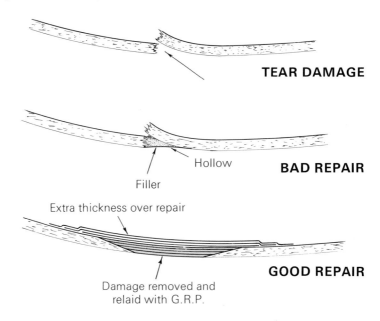

TEAR DAMAGE

Hollow

Filler

BAD REPAIR

Extra thickness over repair

GOOD REPAIR

Damage removed and
relaid with G.R.P.

Structural
Repairs
    I have seen craft with very large sections of hull missing altogether and they have still been repaired to the satisfaction of Lloyd's. In fact most repairs completed under a Lloyd's surveyor are ultimately stronger than the original and are, needless to say, undetectable.

Osmosis
    One of the most popular words to be found whilst talking about G.R.P. troubles is osmosis. I say popular because it covers a multitude of sins; anything out of the ordinary on a gel coat surface often gets the label osmosis whether it is or not. It is a condition where a whole series of blisters appears just below the gel coat covering. In hot weather their contents swell and they appear as bumps, in cold weather they contract and become hollows.

    The cure for this is simple enough although it can be very expensive to put right. Every single little blister must be pierced and taken back to sound material and set aside to dry thoroughly. Once this is done, the open blister can be filled with gel or polyester filling and rubbed back to a good surface then painted.

    The paint system used should be a two-pack polyurethane product such as International 709. Providing that the surface has been etched and correctly primed, this product will produce a finish that is every bit as good as the original.

    There are a number of reputable glass fibre manufacturers who use this system for their new craft. They do not use a pigmented gel at all, instead the whole craft, when complete, is totally painted with a two-pack polyurethane paint.

Lloyd's
Moulding
Release Note

One item that will assure you that the hull of a craft is up to scratch is a Lloyd's Moulding Release Note. This will prove that the craft in question was laid up under the supervision of a Lloyd's surveyor. He makes as many visits during the craft's construction as he sees fit. He will also stick an embossed moulding number into the mould, normally on a dymotape, so that it is actually moulded into the hull of the new craft and is not removable.

He usually leaves the number embossed in the upper starboard side of the transom Fig. 50, although I have seen the number in various other positions on the transom, including at the bottom in the centre. If

Fig 50. Where to look for Registered No.

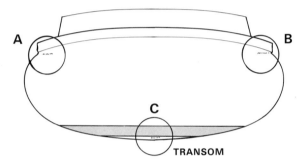

a number is spotted, then you are in luck, because on receipt of that number, Lloyd's Register will be able to supply full information on date of build, laminating company, etc. The very existence of a number assures that the hull has a recorded pedigree. On a cautious note, you may find that the craft's pedigree begins and ends at the moulders, in other words, a Lloyd's approved moulding was purchased by an amateur. I recall such a situation where a private individual lashed out and purchased a very famous class of motor cruiser; he also had the factory install the engines and machinery. All this was done to perfection at considerable cost, and delivered with the various Lloyd's certificates and notes. From that point he fitted it out himself and unashamedly made a 'right pig's ear' of it. Imagine how that craft *could* appear in the brokerage books:

> 35' FAMOUS CLASS T.S.M.C.
> Moulded by . . . to Lloyd's in 197?
> Fitted twin 175HP Perkins Diesels
> Luxuriously fitted out—4 berths
> Very fast SNIP £25,000 ONO

Nothing in that advertisement is untrue, but the words 'moulded to Lloyd's' can fool an unsuspecting prospective purchaser, quite understandably, into thinking the whole craft is built to a very high standard; in fact only the mouldings are to Lloyd's, the rest was a 'tip'. The term 'luxuriously fitted out' is relative and means very little. The

owner's idea of luxury compared with yours, may be poles apart.
    This was a factual craft I saw for myself and, unfortunately, it is not
an isolated case. People with an eye to earning a few quid believe they
can save a large amount of money by doing it themselves or by giving it
to Joe down the street to do for a few bob—he's good at woodwork.
The fact that he has never built a boat before is considered irrelevant.

Moulded Deck   Most hulls that are moulded in G.R.P. have a moulded deck to
match. Often these incorporate the coachroof, cockpit, mast step, toe
rails, and stanchion bases, all in a single moulding. This is a wonderful
innovation so far as a leakproof deck is concerned, as leaks can come
only from holes made in the deck to receive deck fittings and windows
etc. and it is here that trouble can often be found. Badly fitted windows
and hatches will often be the cause of annoying leaks. The only really
satisfactory way of curing them is to remove them completely and start
again. Because it is messy, people tend to skimp on the bedding of
such fittings, when in fact it should be applied generously so that it
squeezes out all round. Many good boatbuilders also introduce a
strand of boat cotton as well for good measure. Another cause of leaks
can be the absence of a sealer around the screws and bolts. A little
extra time spent attending to these details will save the aggravation of
doing the job a second time not to mention the annoyance of a leak.
    The fixing of the deck to the hull is a task that must be securely done.
There is a large variety of different hull/deck join-up systems; the four
most commonly used are illustrated in Fig. 51.

Fig 51. Hull/deck joins.

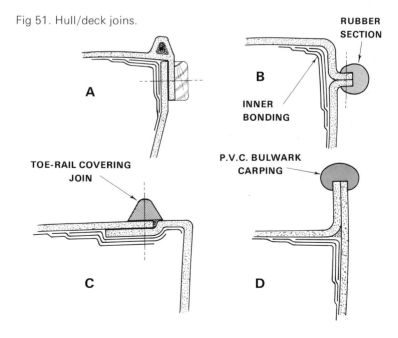

RUBBER
SECTION

A

B

INNER
BONDING

TOE-RAIL COVERING
JOIN

P.V.C. BULWARK
CARPING

C

D

The all have one thing in common and that is they should be securely bolted together and G.R.P. bonded over the actual join on the inside of the hull.

One fault that can occur as a result of skimping in this operation is when the bolts are spaced too far apart. This can be the cause of an undulating sheer-line.

Type 'B' in Fig. 51 is prone to cracking along its upper and lower corners. Fig. 52. This type of damage is normally caused by an impact like hitting the quay wall. This method of join is most often found on the smaller economy type craft. Many boats of this type will be found to be secured with pop rivets, a practice that makes a traditional boatbuilder shudder.

Fig 52. Possible cracks in hull/deck join.

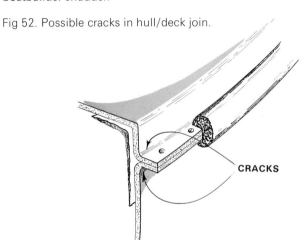

CRACKS

Hand in hand with join-ups go rubbing strakes and fenders. Very often these are incorporated and fitted as a single operation. Most older G.R.P. craft sported a varnished wooden rubbing strake. This gave an attractive relief from the starkness of glass and a clear line to the sheer. Owing to the high cost of timber and the expense of the skilled labour to fit it, many alternatives have appeared. Fig. 53. Indeed some craft do not have a rubbing strip at all. Others are getting smaller and smaller as material costs increase so that many of the modern production-line craft have inadequate rubbing strips.

Hull Distortion   The arrival of all G.R.P. craft has brought problems hitherto unheard of. One such condition is caused by mouldings being removed from their mould before they have cured. Once out of the supporting mould the product can sag and distort and finally cure into obscure shapes. Fig. 54. Although very strong, a G.R.P. hull is very flexible indeed until the deck and bulkheads are fitted. If this flexible hull is left unsupported, trouble will result. If this distortion is not detected and checked it may well be built into the boat. The same applies to the deck.

Fig 53. Methods of fixing rubbing strake.

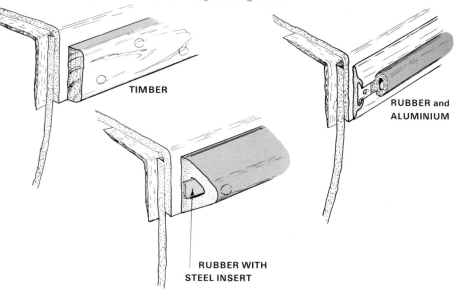

TIMBER

RUBBER and ALUMINIUM

RUBBER WITH STEEL INSERT

Fig 54. Possible distortion of a G.R.P. hull.

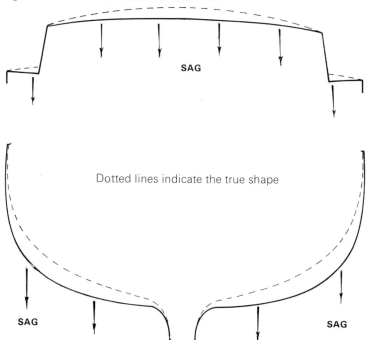

SAG

Dotted lines indicate the true shape

SAG SAG

Maintenance   Despite what the advertisements say, G.R.P. is not a maintenance
and Cleaning free material if you require the maximum from it. It does not need a
G.R.P.   great deal of looking after but does need some. Like the bodywork of a
car, a glass fibre boat needs a good polish-up about twice a year to
keep it in first class order. The polish serves not only to give it that
attractive shine but to repel dirt, grease and maintain its colour. A
silicone free polish should be used; a whole range is available from
your yacht chandler. Frequent freshwater washing is important and
gives that looked-after appearance.

Avoid any cleaners that contain abrasive powders. They will produce
minute scratches and dull the shine. The list below sets out the cleaners
that can be used on G.R.P. surfaces:

Washing-up liquid.	Any soap.
Mild bleach.	Methylated spirit.
Petrol.	Alcohol.
Paraffin.	Turps.
White spirit.	*Polyurethane thinners.
*Carbon tetrachloride.	*Acetone.
*wash off well after use.	

IF IN DOUBT . . . DON'T.

4. On Deck

A high percentage of repairs to wooden craft is in the area of the deck. This is the part that takes the most wear and tear from both the elements and the people who use the boat. An area of constant and varied stress, its timbers are always on the move, expanding and contracting with dry and damp atmospheres, besides drenching seas and blistering sun. In areas such as this the centuries old tradition of the shipwright's craft really shows itself; the complex wooden structure uses the various natural qualities of the different timbers to greatest effect.

The selection of just the right timber for the job is one of the skills the shipwright/boatbuilder has to have at his fingertips; he not only searches out the correct type of timber but also the condition, seasoned or green, straight grained or curly, knotty or clean. Each one of these factors he will use to its best advantage and he must also make allowances for the timber to expand or contract; neglect of any one of these points could mean a split or bow in the resulting job.

Many have the impression that boats built of hardwood are superior to those built of softwood, but this is not necessarily true. The difference between hardwood and softwood has little bearing on quality; many fine traditional craft built with softwood, say pitch pine or larch, are still to be found in perfect condition, perhaps having clocked-up a hundred years or so of service. The technical difference between hardwood and softwood is that hardwood trees shed their leaves in winter (deciduous), whilst softwood trees (coniferous) are generally of the narrow leafed pine type. It is interesting to note that balsa wood, although very soft by nature, is in fact a hardwood.

Appendix I—Hardwoods—and Appendix II—Softwoods—give some of the details, qualities and use of timber commonly employed in the building of boats. It must be remembered that even when the hull is constructed of some other material, various types of wood are usually used in turning the bare hull into a completed boat.

Decks

There are many items distributed throughout the deck that exert considerable stresses upon the structure; mast, rigging, stanchions, cleats and winches all must be able to work with the timber yet at the same time remain watertight.

Traditionally the deck of a yacht was laid directly upon the beams, Fig. 55, and relied totally upon the craftsman's skill to produce a watertight job. He had to allow just the right amount of seam for caulking since that kept the water out. Each plank of the decking is made so that the lower edges meet whilst the outer edges form a seam into which the caulking is fitted. This can be done by shaping both edges of the plank Fig. 56A, or by chamfering only one. The depth of the caulking seam is about two-thirds of the thickness of the decking itself.

Fig 55. Traditionally laid deck.

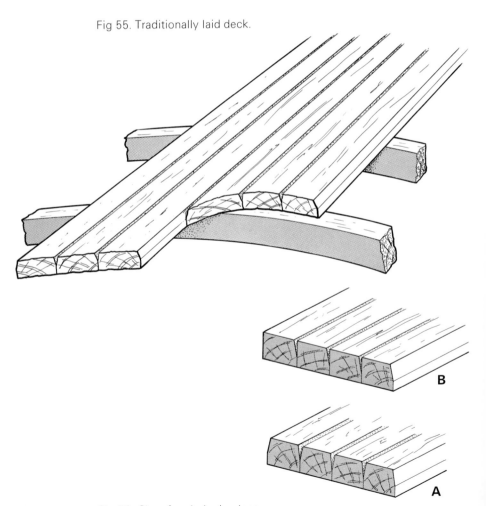

B

A

Fig 56. Chamfered plank edges.

Seams were normally caulked with oakum or boat cotton which had to be driven home with just the right amount of force; too loose and the seam would leak, too hard would drive the caulking right through. This is a fault that may be spotted when looking at the undersides of some traditionally laid decks and often referred to as curtains.

Another more commonly used method of producing a laid deck is to fit a marine plywood skin over the beams first. This gives a positive waterproof layer, then the decking is laid on top of the plywood in the normal way. Fig. 57. Where this method is used the decking itself would not normally be as thick.

Fig 57. Decking laid over plywood.

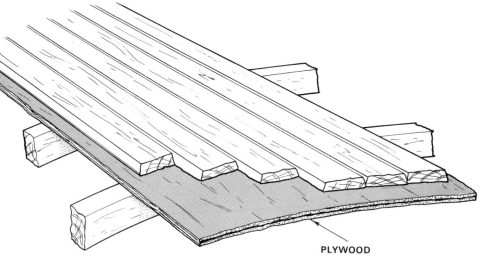

PLYWOOD

The deck was then payed-up with pitch or Jeffery's marine glue which gave the black seams we associate with laid decks. Applying these products required the pitch or the Jeffery's to be heated up in a pitch-pot until liquid and then payed into the seams with a heated ladle. Fig. 58. Once cooled the surplus could be scraped off and the decks swept clean.

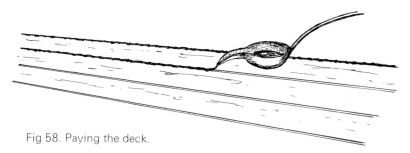

Fig 58. Paying the deck.

There are now far more advanced products available that are easier and cleaner to use. Normally of a two-pack type that do not require heating and are supplied in a container designed to deliver the mixture directly into the seam with the minimum of fuss.

Laid or bright decks can follow one of two types. Fig. 59. Straight decking where each plank runs parallel to the ship's centre-line, or curved decking that follows the line of the gunwale. For curved decking each plank has to be set-on-edge to follow the gunwale, which is a very skilled and labour-intensive procedure, hence it is the most expensive.

On a yacht or motor cruiser the king plank and covering board would be varnished whilst the decking itself is left untreated save for its caulking. If the decks are teak, as they most often are, they need only to be kept scrubbed to produce that white impeccable appearance.

Fig 55. Decks can be laid straight (A) or curved to follow the line of the gunwale (B).

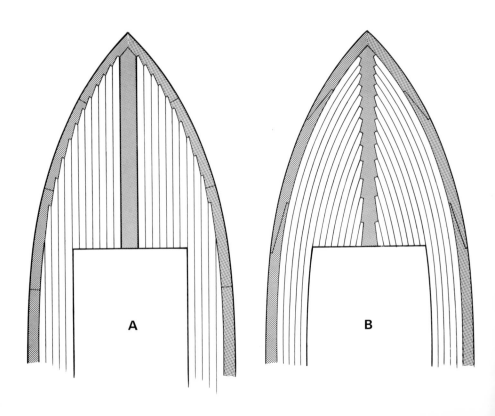

A   B

There are two main methods of securing a laid deck. Fig. 60. Hidden nailed—where the planks are copper nailed through their sides and the edge of each plank covers the fixings of the last. Doweled—where the planks are counter-bored, screwed and then doweled. If the dowels are made from the same timber as the decking and fitted with their grain running in the same direction, they should be inconspicuous.

The former gives the most attractive results since none of the fixings are visible. The reader may encounter a mixture of both of the two methods described here. Some builders use the edge nailed method but dowel and screw the decking into the beams.

Whilst examining laid decks one may spot small shaped pieces of timber let-in the planks. These are 'little shipwrights'. They are in fact little patches covering a small area of damage that did not warrant removing a whole length of decking.

One other traditional method of decking was to cover the planking with canvas and paint, which is also a perfectly acceptable method. Areas to watch for are hatch surrounds and openings besides all edges. These are normally sealed by the fitting of a beading or quadrant. Fig. 61. It is in these areas that the painted canvas can begin to crack

Fig 60. Laid decks may be secured by hidden nailing (A) or dowelled (B).

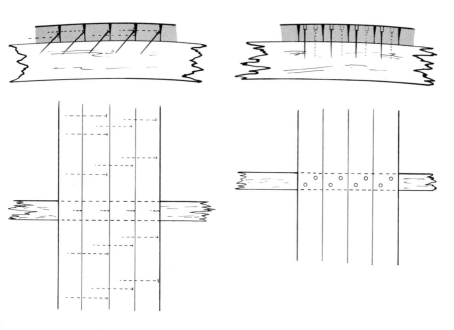

A   B

and let the water in. Look also for chaffing or holes in the canvas as this is not easy to repair successfully. Once the canvas has been holed and water penetrates beneath we have all the ingredients required for rot to set in. Paint and canvased decks can be perfectly acceptable but they can also be covering a multitude of sins.

Fig 61. Areas to watch with deck covered by canvas and paint.

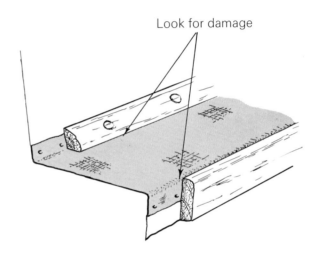

Look for damage

Sheathed Decks

Be very wary of decks, particularly on older craft, that are sheathed in glass fibre. The same reasons apply as mentioned in Chapter 2, Sheathing a hull, and to have any chance of success at all G.R.P. sheathing should have all its edges securely bedded and fixed under a timber batten or beading. If this is not done the edge of the G.R.P. will curl-up and lift allowing water to penetrate between the two.

Not to be confused with glass fibre, cascovered decks are quite a different thing. Cascover is a closely woven nylon fabric that is secured to the timber with a resorcinol glue. Carried out correctly this method could actually enhance the price of a boat; it can be very strong and long lasting providing it was applied to sound timber under the correct conditions in the first place. Many wooden boats are sheathed with this whilst they are being built and it often lasts the life of the boat.

One reason why this method of sheathing has a greater chance of success than glass fibre is that the resorcinol glue is manufactured to glue timber whereas glass fibre is not.

Any type of sheathing may well remain sound on the outside but that does not ensure that the timber underneath will stay in the same condition. Cutting off a supply of air to the timber can sometimes be the cause of rot. So even if a deck seems to be sound on the outside don't forget to have a good look on the inside as well.

Coachroofs and Coamings   Areas where coachroof and coamings join to decks also need a good coat-of-looking-at. Varnishwork will often reveal damp and blackened timber; rotting beadings could spell expensive trouble, Fig. 62. Areas where varnishwork has perished but not stained the timber could mean that only a good varnishing job is required to bring it up to scratch; but left too long the timber underneath will become wet and begin to discolour or even rot.

Fig 62. Points to check on the coachroof.

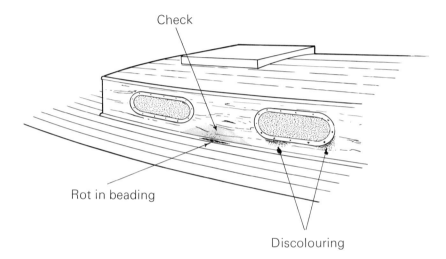

Check

Rot in beading

Discolouring

Port Lights and Windows   Look closely at port lights, deck lights and windows. These may require removing and cleaning-up, even re-chroming. Deck lights, Fig. 63, may be encountered let neatly in the decks of the older type of craft. Treat these with care. At one time a deck light was a standard

Fig 63. Deck light fitting.

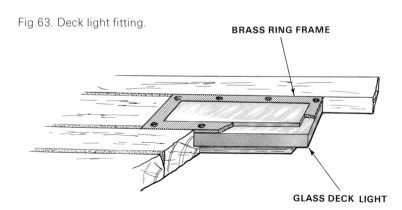

BRASS RING FRAME

GLASS DECK LIGHT

chandlery item available almost anywhere, but now I suspect you would have some difficulty finding a replacement. If a prism were found to be cracked or leaking a replacement may have to be a piece of heavy plate glass.

An opening portlight, Fig. 64, called a scuttle, may require its sealing gasket to be replaced. These are normally made of a hard neoprene type rubber. If the glass itself is cracked or needs replacement this can be done by unscrewing the inner, normally brass, ring. Again replacement portlight glass was once a standard item of chandlery but now one would have to depend on a glazier to cut one.

Portlights on larger craft may be fitted with deadlights and these too are fitted with a sealing gasket. Replacement is as described above for portlights.

Fig 64. Opening port light or scuttle with dead light.

Aluminium framed windows should be anodized. If they are not the window frames will corrode and waste very quickly in the salt atmosphere. Any cracked or broken glass in this type of frame is a job for the professional since they should be properly sealed and the correct type of safety glass used.

All boat windows should be made of a safety glass; ordinary household plate glass is very dangerous indeed, since when it breaks the result is wickedly jagged spikes of glass.

Avoid any windows that are fitted with perspex. These scratch very easily and even after some short service, in a sea water atmosphere, will craze and generally become opaque and need replacing frequently. New special types of plastic window material are finding their way onto the marine market; one in particular, developed for the racing car market, is reputed to be unbreakable, scratch resistant and extremely tough. It is already in production with several new boats and no doubt will become more popular and widely used as time goes by and its price comes down.

eck Fittings   Check chainplates for trouble. Fig. 65. The first point to look for is wear. The point where the clevis pin of the bottlescrew or shackle bears on the chainplate may reveal a wastage of metal. Another thing to check is that there has been no movement for'd and aft of the plates, which will prove whether the retaining bolts are tight; this is often revealed by a slight scuffing either side, even a broken paint joint may give a clue. Rust marks under and around the fixing bolts should invite you to have one removed for a closer inspection. This can be caused simply by the galvanizing breaking down; it would probably be as cheap to replace the bolts as to pay for the old ones to be cleaned-up and regalvanized.

Fig 65. Possible chainplate problems.

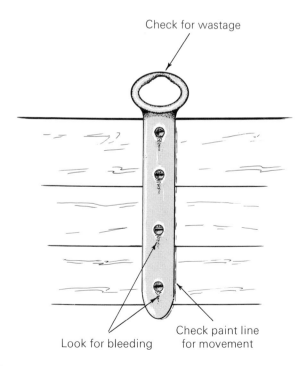

Check for wastage

Look for bleeding   Check paint line for movement

Look at the stem-head roller in a similar way. Check that the hole for the fore-stay fitting has not become elongated and worn. Look also at the pin that runs through the centre of the roller and check for wear.

An examination of the cleats should follow a similar line. Keep an eye open for any missing fitting. A missing cleat for instance, can indicate all manner of problems; was it removed or was it dragged off? If the latter is true then more extensive damage can be sought.

Cleats should always be secured by through bolts using a large pad on the underside of the deck to help distribute the loads. Fig. 66. The bolts should also have a twist of boat cotton and bedding around their heads before being hauled up tight.

Fig 66. Method of securing a cleat.

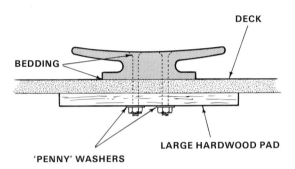

A stanchion base is where trouble often occurs. The poor old stanchion is one of the most abused items on deck; its object is to support a lifeline for those on deck and in this role it would give long and trouble free service. The trouble starts when it is used as a lever for people to haul themselves aboard from the jetty or dinghy. Imagine the enormous load transmitted down through the stanchion to its fixings on the deck. It's in this area that trouble is most often encountered.

It is a wise move to back-out one or two of the holding down bolts in the stanchion bases. Take them out from different places, say one on the inboard side of the base and on another base the outboard one. It is very important that this item is right and that the fixings are good as the only time they are really going to be put to the test is when a life will depend upon it.

It is quite common to find that the outboard fixing will turn out to be a screw. This is not good practice, but the reason a screw is sometimes used in this place is simply that it is difficult to get a bolt through at that spot due to the gunwale beneath. If the remainder of the fixings in that base are good sound through bolts and the odd screw is holding well, it could be accepted but only if the other fixings are bolts.

This is an area that often produced leaks. Closer examination of the adjoining area beneath the foot will often give you a clue to this where the nut and washer has started to disappear up into the timber. Larger washers is the obvious first cure, but if the timber in that area is waterlogged or rotten the repair bill could be very high indeed. So have a good prod around in this area. Fig. 67.

Fig 67. Area of stanchion base.

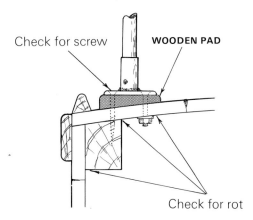

Where the stanchion base is on a pad check that it is not split, which is another cause of leaks. It may be gummed-up with mastic or putty, but if it still leaks the only sure way to fix it is to renew the pad.

Handrails are another item that must be through bolted. In fact I have a general rule that is 'If life could depend on it—Bolt it', and handrails are no exception.

Mast Steps   If the craft is a sailing boat the base of the mast will need looking at. There are two main types: (a) A mast that is stepped in a tabernacle on deck. (b) A mast that passes through the deck into a step in the keel.

The tabernacle stepped on deck makes lowering the stick much easier, Fig. 68, as it is in fact a hinge. Often the tabernacle fitting itself is

Fig 68. Tabernacle mast step.

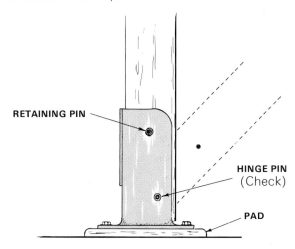

made in mild steel and galvanized; damaged galvanizing will show itself with traces of rust down the fitting and adjoining area. Look closely at the two large bolts that hold the mast in position; on some craft the mast hinges on the upper bolt, on others the lower. The bolt to examine is the one that the mast is hinged on; it seldom gets removed so is the most suspect.

As with the stanchions check below decks to see that the whole thing is securely fitted to a good sized pad or you may find it combined with a heavy post that delivers the load directly to the keel.

A mast that is stepped in the keel is more likely to leak as it passes through the deck; here will be found mast wedges, which in turn are covered with a mast coat. Fig. 69. If possible lift the mast coat and check beneath with a spike or hammer. This is an area that spends most of its life covered and if the coat has let any water pass then there is the possibility of rot.

A traditional craft will be fitted with more elaborate mast wedges. Fig. 70. They are skilfully made by the shipwright in much the same

Fig 69. Mast stepped on the keel.

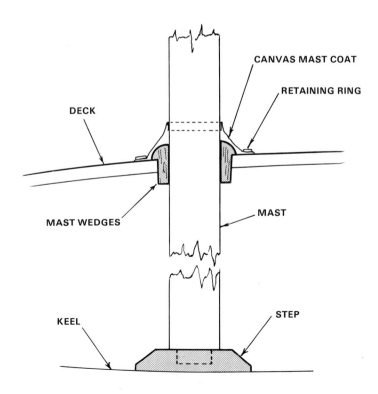

way as the cooper's barrel; each one formed to a slight wedge on one side whilst snuggly fitting the mast on the other. Some older masts were made with an octagonal section where they passed through the deck, which made the fitting of mast wedges much easier. Once in position the mast wedges were then caulked to produce a watertight job, and then the mast coat fitted over the lot to finish it.

Look closely for any 'little shipwrights' let into the mast. This can reveal that rot has already shown itself and has been treated. In this case check around the repairs to make sure the trouble was thoroughly dealt with in the first place. If everything is thickly coated with paint use the hammer to sound it out.

One point of interest, if the boat has the mast unshipped have a look with a torch in the mast step. Scrape aside any dirt and you may find the imprint of a coin, or you may even be lucky enough to find the coin itself. It was an old custom and considered lucky to place a golden sovereign beneath the heel of the mast. It is rare to find the golden sovereign but I have often seen the imprint left by one.

Fig 70. Mast wedges.

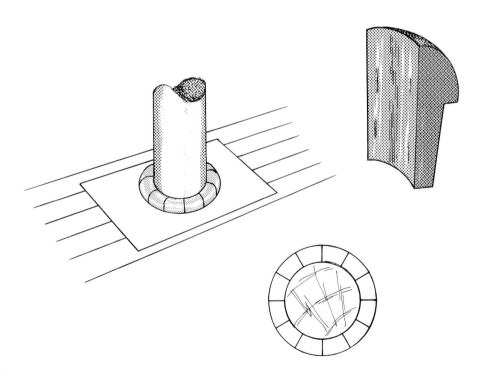

Deck
Openings

Companionways, doors, hatches and skylights are areas where leaks often occur. Let's look at some of them and their problems.

Older craft may well be fitted with beautiful skylights. Fig. 71A. These are complex pieces of joinery and very difficult to build so that they open and close yet remain watertight. They are seen less and less on new boats these days and to have one replaced would be very expensive indeed, that is assuming a craftsman was available who knew how to build one.

Sliding hatches vary greatly in their construction. Fig. 71B. The most successful is probably the type that used brass runners. Some rely on two surfaces of timber as runners but these usually stick and become troublesome as they grow older. A rub of beeswax or beeswax and candlegrease on the running surfaces will help this situation.

Cabin doors are just about as varied. These can range from a simple but effective drop-in panel type, Fig. 71D, on a small sailing cruiser, to beautifully joinered double teak doors. Fig. 71C. Not seen so often on modern boats, these heavy doors were sometimes fitted with lift-off hinges so that they could be removed and stowed below when not required.

Modern hatches are normally of anodized aluminium and toughened glass; these come in two main types, the super heavily built model with

Fig 71. Deck openings.

good large clamps to really draw them down to a watertight fit, or the cheaper extruded aluminium type that just clip down onto a rubber gasket. One problem often encountered with the cheaper type, and very often the cause of a leak, is the joint between extrusions. The same can be true for the spot where the ends of the rubber gasket join. The manufacturers normally position these joins directly below one of the hinges to be least conspicuous; so when searching for a leak from inside it looks, often wrongly, as though the hinge is at fault.

One repair I have used successfully is to 'V' out the dry aluminium join and run a line of silicon sealer into it. This normally does the trick although I am surprised that the makers have not yet come to terms with this fault.

Lastly, on deck you will encounter ventilators of some type, pretty insignificant items, but of critical importance. One of the biggest single causes of rot in a wooden boat is lack of ventilation. They should be of good size and positioned so there is a free passage of air throughout the boat. Fig. 72 gives an idea of some of the various different types that may be encountered.

Fig 72. Varieties of ventilators.

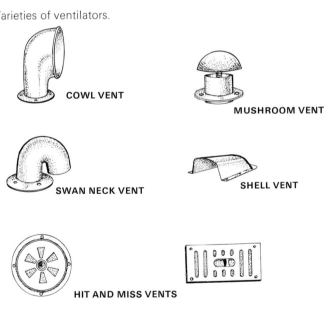

COWL VENT

MUSHROOM VENT

SWAN NECK VENT

SHELL VENT

HIT AND MISS VENTS

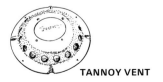

TANNOY VENT

FLEXIBLE COWL VENT

Liferafts   On a well found yacht you will probably find an inflatable liferaft. These are usually encased within a glass fibre container and stowed in a convenient place on deck. They are an expensive item that can enhance the value of a boat and its safety factor, but they must be serviced and checked regularly. On the glass fibre canister will be found details of servicing history; if you find its last service was several years ago then its value is not so high because it will need a major and expensive overhaul.

I remember surveying a motor cruiser with a liferaft container on deck, and I was more than a little surprised to discover that there was no liferaft at all inside it. This, in my opinion, is criminal because the first time you would require its use could be in an emergency. Imagine the dilemma it would cause if you had to leave your ship only to find that what had appeared to be the liferaft was not one at all but two empty shells placed together.

Having said that I have also checked liferafts that have not been serviced for 10 years or so and on returning them to the manufacturers, who have pulled the cord they have worked perfectly. The standard is very high indeed, so too are the regulations regarding their service and maintenance. If you make offshore or open sea passages it is in your own interest that such items are kept up to scratch. Whilst on the subject of safety distress flares too are printed with an expiry date. Make sure these are in order.

Anchors   Most sea-going craft are equipped with two anchors, normally of different types, perhaps a C.Q.R. or Danforth type as the main anchor and a fisherman as a stand-by. Fig. 73. The anchors are pretty robust items but, like chain or warp, they are only as strong as their weakest link. So any chain or warp should be flaked out and inspected closely. Check the first and last links and the shackles for wear. If the chain is rusty then check even more closely.

Once the chain is out of the locker pop your head inside and have a look. See what happens to the water and mud that comes onboard with the chain. The chain locker should be well drained. Look also to see if the end of the anchor chain is secured. It should be secured to an eyebolt or the like by a length of stout line and not shackled. The reason is that should ever an emergency arise that requires you to let go the anchor cable altogether, the chances are you will need to do it in a hurry and a shackle would probably be rusted-up or stuck while a line can easily be cut.

Fig 73. Types of anchor commonly used in boats.

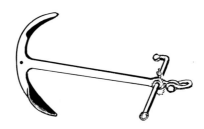

FISHERMAN

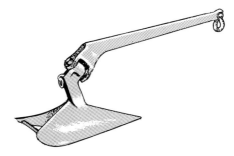

C.Q.R.

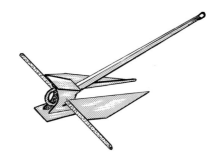

MEON/DANFORTH

5. Look below

Below decks can reveal a whole world of woodworking craftsmanship and laminating skills; the cleverly shaped timberwork of the planking, timbers, knees, floors and stringers are all to be found. It is all there to be examined if we know what to look for and where. We can also tell much about the quality of laminating; dry mat with areas of razor-sharp glass fibre needles sticking up is no recommendation. On G.R.P. craft a check should be made on the bonding of bulkheads and structural members to the hull; a common fault is where the G.R.P. bonding parts from the timber. See Fig. 78B. I have also seen many craft where important structures are not bonded at all or at best merely tacked in short areas. Look up under the side decks at the hull/deck join; this should be securely bonded one to the other.

In addition to the structure, there is the joinery; doors, stairs, lockers and drawers each hold clues and reflections on the men who made and owned the craft. Let's look at the structure first.

Down below in a traditionally built wooden boat can be dark, since glass was treated with great respect and kept to the very minimum. This, in the main, was because anything to do with glass meant a possible leak. Toughened glass was at one time unknown while ordinary household type glass was fragile. So a lead lamp or good torch is essential for a good inspection.

Damp
As you go below for the first time literally have a good sniff around; if the cabin smell is fousty and damp it could give you a clue that the boat has been locked-up for some time with little or no ventilation, which might well have started rot. Where cushions and soft furnishings are still aboard, handle them to see if the material is rotten or damp; cushion covers and curtains can be very costly to replace quite apart from the trouble their condition can indicate.

Where books and charts are still aboard check that the paper is still crisp and dry; dampness would show itself very quickly here leaving the paper limp and heavy. G.R.P. boats sometimes have a condensation problem which can lead to staining of timberwork, particularly plywood, and even to rot.

Hidden Clues   As I have already mentioned in a previous chapter, much of the craft's structure may well be covered with joinery and hidden from view; in such cases it can be of enormous help to know what goes where. But let us have a rummage to see what we can find.

The cabin sole of older wooden craft is often boarded in rather like the floor of a house, although tongued and grooved timber is not normally found. Remove any carpets or covering on the sole, and this should reveal a series of hatches along its centre. It is through these that we can check keel bolts, floors, keel and planking.

The first sight below will tell you whether the bilges have received any attention or not. If the sole plates or hatches are difficult to get up it will indicate that they have not been removed very much, causing an ideal situation for rot. All these little snippets of information, if noted, will help to compile a pretty accurate idea of how well the boat has been looked after.

If everything in the bilges is caked with the grime of ages it will be obvious that they have received little or no attention. Rusting water will indicate that some galvanizing somewhere has broken down and that the limber holes are blocked. On the other hand I have seen bilges that have been as immaculately kept as the topsides, some varnished, some even painted white. These are a treat to look at and obviously the pride of a meticulous and caring owner.

Floors   Check over the floors and if possible remove one or two bolts for checking whilst you are at it. There are many different types of floors. Fig. 74A. Galvanized iron is a good common type of fitting. The main type of trouble encountered here is a breakdown in the galvanizing. This reveals itself by heavy rust deposits and flaking paint. The centre bolt through the floor is often also a keel bolt and worth closer inspection. Fig. 74B. Grown timber floors are very often found in heavy fishing or working type boats, and are the oldest and most traditional

Fig 74. Types of floor in boat construction.

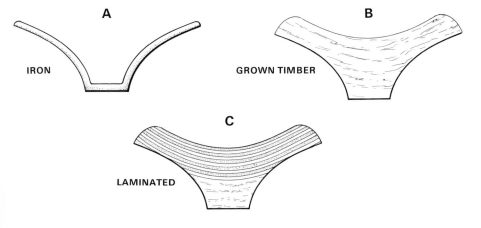

A

IRON

B

GROWN TIMBER

C

LAMINATED

method. Shaped floors were often cut from crooks of naturally grown timber, and trouble with this type of floor is mainly from splitting. Fig. 74C. Laminated floors are comparatively new. So if an old Gaffer has a series of laminated floors throughout her bottom the chances are they would be a replacement or an addition to the original. Laminated members are standard practice in more modern boatbuilding and probably produces the best job of all.

Where the floors are bolted through the keel the width of a wooden floor should be about three to three and a half times the diameter of the bolt. This is a rule of thumb but illustrates that to be effective a wooden floor must be a chunky piece of timber. So if a 1 in. keel bolt passes through it the floor should be at least 3 in. wide.

The object of the floor is to tie the structure of the boat together, one side to another, and strength in this depends upon the fixings. Very seldom was glue or adhesive ever used in the structure of an old boat; other than caulking and white or red lead, sealing the craft depended on fixings and the boatbuilder's skill. On a craft built to Lloyd's specification floors should be attached with a minimum of three fastenings along each arm and two across the throat.

Floors on G.R.P. craft are integrally laminated structures similar in shape to those already mentioned, and sometimes forming short bulkheads or partitions throughout the bilge.

Bilges   Whilst in the bilges check all the timber in sight, inside of planking, keel, timbers, grown frames, stem and stern post. Use the bradawl to poke around and concentrate on joins and corners. Fig. 75. Rot often tends to start in a corner, on an edge or around a bolt. Keep an eye open for broken and cracked timbers, cracked frames and knees; beam shelf, stringers, carlins and deck beams all ought to be examined as closely as possible. The areas to search out are the least accessible and not just the parts that are easily to hand. Remember that you are out looking for trouble, so don't kid yourself that none exists. Look along edges, on corners, around joints and bolts, in crooks and crannies; these inaccessible areas are also the most expensive for repairs since whole areas of the boat may have to be removed to get at the affected spots.

It is important that limber holes are kept free to prevent water from laying in pockets throughout the bilges. You may come across boats with a length of very light chain running through the bilges passing through each of the limber holes; this is a device to keep the holes clear. Just a wiggle on the chain and they are all cleared out together.

In the engine room area limber holes are equally important, so too is a sump tray under the engine to prevent leaking oil from running into the bilges. On a G.R.P. craft the sump tray may be a sealed section beneath the engine. These are normally gelled on the inside to prevent any ingress of oil into the laminates of the hull.

In the business end of the boat, where the stern tube is situated, pay particular attention to any areas that may have received damage through vibration. Engine bearers are often through bolted to the outside of the planking and any looseness is sometimes given away by

Fig 75. Points to look for in the bilges.

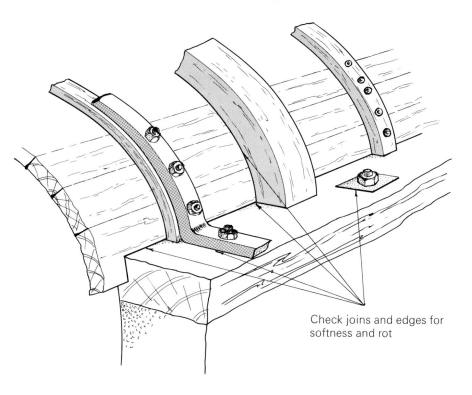

Check joins and edges for
softness and rot

tell-tale wet marks on the outside of the hull. As with most items that
live in the bilges this structural timberwork may well be coated with the
grime of ages, plus a good many coats of paint. The bradawl will be
needed to penetrate the paint if the timber is to be checked.

Engine Beds   The engine can be held down onto its beds in a wooden boat by a
variety of ways. Fig. 76. On a G.R.P. craft the engine beds will probably
be integrally moulded into the hull, and although the principle for
holding the engine down remains the same as in a wooden boat, there
are variations. Fig. 77. Another method used on some craft is a
combination of both. The engine beds, usually of heavy plywood, are
glassed into position. Fig. 78. This is perfectly adequate providing a
check is kept on the bond of the beds to the hull. the tell-tale signs
begin with a small gap appearing between the wooden beds and the
bonding. Fig. 78B. It is not the end of the world if this does happen but
remedial work with the engine, piping and wiring all in place can be
very involved and in turn expensive.

Fig 76. Securing engine to bed in wooden boat.

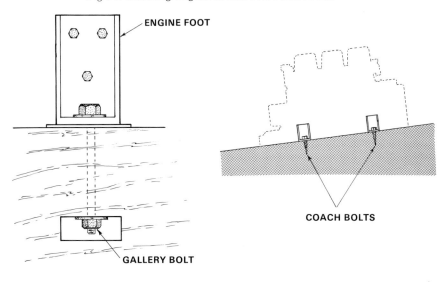

ENGINE FOOT

COACH BOLTS

GALLERY BOLT

Fig 77. Securing engine to beds in G.R.P. craft.

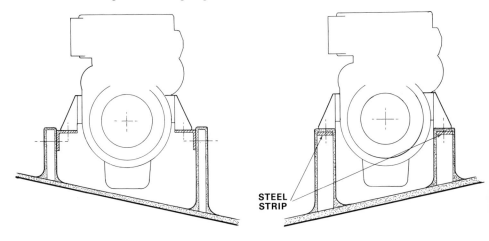

STEEL STRIP

If the boat is out of the water the shaft couplings should be broken to avoid any strains being transmitted to the line-up as the craft absorbs the stresses of being hauled or lifted out. The line-up can be checked at this stage but if the boat is blocked off under stress it could be temporarily out of line. So the check on engine alignment would be most sensibly done with the craft afloat before the two couplings are bolted together.

Whilst on the subject of engine line-up I will just mention three

Fig 78. Wooden engine beds glassed into the hull.

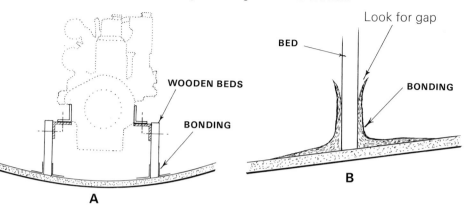

A

B

Fig 79. Methods of aligning engine with shaft.

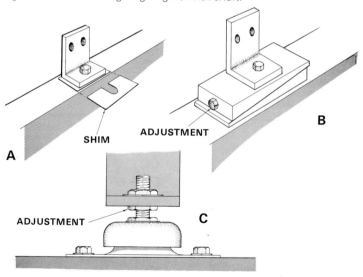

A

B

C

methods of adjusting the engine's position to bring it into perfect
alignment with the shaft. Fig. 79. The most basic method is to fit
slithers (shims) of tin or brass under the feet of the engine to achieve
the correct height. Fig. 79B. A pair of interlocking metal wedges that
are adjustable by means of a nut either end is another method.
Fig. 79C. The more modern method of adjustment is using flexible
mounts; these have an adjusting nut on each of the feet, which makes
the final line-up easy.

Skin Fittings

Skin fittings on a wooden craft are often secured through a pad on the inside. Have a prod around this area. The skin-fittings themselves are often items that become sadly neglected. A common and bad practice that can cause trouble is that owners often leave their seacocks turned 'ON'. These then seize-up in the open position and will not close. This problem is common where seacocks are situated in a position that is difficult or awkward to get at and out of laziness the owner just does not bother to turn them off. The result is the fitting soon seizes solid. So, if the seacocks and toilet skin-fittings are tucked away, search them out and give them a good-coat-of-looking-at.

There are two main patterns of seacocks. Fig. 80. The screw-up gate valve type (A). These in general are trouble free and put in good service of years. The lever type (B) operates by turning a lever half a turn one way or the other. This is the type that will seize-up if not kept in use or well serviced. These work on a tapered cone system and if too loose or pitted will leak, too tight and it will not move. A useful tip that will tell if the fitting is turned on or off; for on, the handle should point to the direction of FLOW. Fig. 81.

If the craft is out of the water it is an easy enough matter to reseat the taper by simply working it in by using a grinding paste, rather like grinding-in a valve. Clean off any traces of grinding paste after use. A smear of waterproof grease before assembly will help things to turn smoothly. Before condemning this type of valve as seized-up, the two retaining bolts (normally one on each side of the lever) should be released. These screws or bolts apply the tension to the cone; too tight and the lever will lock solid, too loose and it will leak.

Fig 80. Two types of seacock.

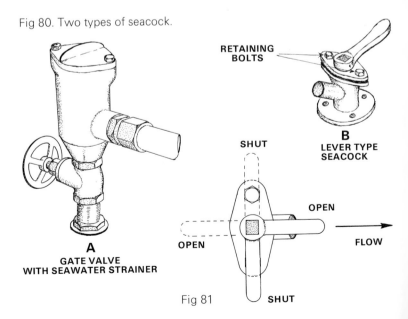

Fig 81

More obvious points to note are rusting pipe or jubilee clips. Check any flexible piping for deterioration and cracking. Engine hoses are prone to decaying and splitting; spares should be carried for these since, just like in the car, they often go in the most inconvenient places.

Engine Look over the engine for oil leaks. You do not have to be a mechanic to spot those and the evidence of oil leaks will indicate the lack of servicing to the engine.

If there is even the slightest suggestion of the engine having been soaked with water, have a jar of the sump oil removed. This should tell you at a glance, providing the sample came from the bottom of the sump, if there is any water present. Oil will float on the water so revealing itself very quickly. If water is present or the oil emulsified it could spell expensive trouble. A more expert, independent, surveyor should be called in.

A surprising amount of repair bills in the engine room area are directly or indirectly the result of insufficient use. This may sound strange but it is true. Even more so where petrol engines are used and older engines with magnetos; both of these deteriorate very quickly in the salty, damp marine atmosphere if not kept well serviced and/or used.

The best way to check over an engine is to run it properly. Then an engineer can hear a good deal. The ability to do this requires a great deal of skill and I do not recommend the reader to draw his conclusion from this. Diesel engines are notoriously noisy machines and it takes the engineer's skills to analyze it. He will even be interested in the exhaust fumes, for so much can be learned from that. Is it blue or black smoke? Each one tells its own story. Table 5. The conditions illustrated

Table 5. Diesel engine exhaust.

No smoke	Engine working correctly	
Black smoke	Too much fuel	Check injectors Check fuel pump Overloaded propeller too big
Blue smoke (under light load)	Injectors	
Blue smoke (under normal working conditions)	Piston rings sticking or broken Valve guides worn Too much oil in sump Faulty engine breathing system Can mean a worn out engine	

should not be judged until the engine is hot and at its working temperature, but to do that the boat must be afloat and running under load.

If the craft is not in the water what can you do? You cannot run the engine under load, that is for sure, but you could turn on the ignition and see if the starter engages and turns the engine over. Whilst doing this, if the engine does fire and start-up then simply turn it off again quickly. No harm can be done in turning an engine over for a second or so but prolonged periods can damage the impellers.

Electrics

One item that is very difficult to check thoroughly is the ship's wiring. The only real way of checking it successfully is to turn everything on to see if it works. Like most things electrical it does not like wet and damp conditions. This is one of the reasons why diesel engines make so much more sense in a boat than petrol engines. The latter is totally dependent upon its delicate electrical ignitions system. One bead of damp or dirt bridging that tiny gap across the ignition points renders the whole propulsion unit useless. So maintenance and servicing are very important.

The batteries are often neglected, as all the time they are working properly the tendency is to leave well alone. It is quite common to find batteries with great clumps of corrosion verdigris around the terminals solely the result of neglect. This corrosive build-up continues until the poor old battery just cannot supply enough power. The engines will not start, lights are dim or out altogether, electric pumps have not got enough energy to turn over and so on.

A kettle of near boiling water over the corroded terminals will quickly clear that, then after drying the terminals, they can be given a coat of petroleum jelly or grease to keep the problem at bay.

Batteries themselves are expensive items and should demand more attention than they normally get. Cracks and chips in the casing are common enough, loose terminals indicate misuse and could render the battery useless. Fig. 82.

Fig 82. Possible defects in the battery.

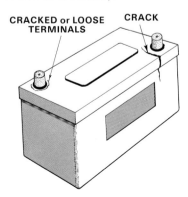

CRACKED or LOOSE   CRACK
TERMINALS

The most common installation uses two batteries, one wired to the engine circuit, the other to the auxiliary supplies. This method always keeps the engine battery fully charged so that if you sit-up reading half the night with the lights on, or leave something switched on, one battery remains fully charged to start-up the engine.

A cross-over switch is wired into the system so that the engine, when running, charges both batteries. The size of the batteries naturally depend upon the power requirement but heavy duty batteries should always be used. They should be fitted in an acid-proof lined box with a lid and vented to fresh air to escort any inflammable gases safely away. Very important also is that a battery master switch be fitted to disconnect the whole electrical circuitry from the batteries. This switch is best fitted in an easy-to-get-at position, if not it will not get switched off.

Joinery

Loosely speaking there are two types of joinery. There is the basic rough but strong type produced by the workboat and fisherman type of builder and secondly there is the genuine craftsman produced items that one would expect to find on a high quality yacht. There are varying degrees of each, e.g. high quality workboats and poor quality yachts. It can also be said that although beautiful and expensive joinery is a joy to look at, very often the more basic simplicity of the working boat has just as much appeal. The main thing is does it work? After all, a door made from a simple piece of plywood that shuts correctly must be better than a joinery made door where the joints come adrift so it no longer shuts at all.

Let us look at some of the items to be found down below in a little more detail. A simple item that can be revealing is the companionway steps. Fig. 83. The good quality joinery job should have the treads of the steps set into the rails with wedged tenons to secure them. Even more elaborate jobs with mouldings incorporated in the treads and risers or even gratings set into the treads may be encountered. Some utilize the bottom step as a locker. Fig. 84.

Fig 83. Companionway steps of   Fig 84. Bottom step used as locker.
good quality joinery.

The more basic version of the same step would be a simple plywood one with the treads sitting on wooden supports. Fig. 85. Although this type is by far the cheapest to construct it still does all the things the expensive joiner made job does. It reflects the basic workmanlike thinking of why-pay-more.

Fig 85. Plywood companionway steps.

TREAD SUPPORTS

Locker fronts share a similarity with the steps. A traditional yacht or motor cruiser may well sport beautiful fronts with mitred panels and beadings, Fig. 86, whilst simple plywood veneered blockboard fronts may be found on the economy class job, Fig. 87. Skilfully done the latter may well be perfectly acceptable and even attractive.

Beadings, mouldings and dovetailed joints are all evidence of the joiner's skill and can be seen with half an eye but, strangely, it does not always mean that the craft is worth more money; although, if you have your quota of sea water in your veins, you will enjoy having it around you. You may encounter beautiful turning work, this style passes in and out of fashion as the years go by. Again it need not add to the value of the boat as a whole but I think there is something distinctive and very nice about it.

Fig 86. Locker doors with   Fig 87. Plywood locker doors.
mitred panels and beadings.

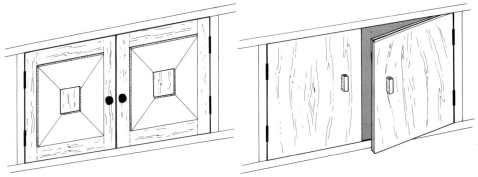

6. Conversions

The very sound of the word conversion can cause many boating people to turn-up their noses and many a craft with that name in the title is tabooed to begin with. The reasons are easy to see when an inspection of some converted craft is made and abortive efforts to transform ships' lifeboats into yachts is probably the most common; however, the spectrum of converted craft is very wide.

Whilst many home built conversions have a hideous almost rustic appearance there are far more good jobs than one at first sight imagines. Good conversions are not as conspicuous and the percentage of good to bad becomes very distorted. Many are professional jobs that would grace the highest standards, craft that have taken on a new lease of life under the loving care of an experienced man.

Many failures are due to lack of experience or understanding and often they are the owners' first boat. The basic logic of their thinking is 'What could be safer than a lifeboat?' No doubt about it, a ship's lifeboat is a very safe craft, but add a high freeboard cabin as most people want full standing headroom, besides an engine and all the equipment that goes with it, then most of the lifeboat's qualities will have disappeared. The weight, displacement and stability are all drastically changed and not always for the good.

Lifeboats designed to be pulled by oars are not built with the structure to take an engine, nor is the keel of suitable size to allow a large stern tube to be bored through it. I have seen craft where the stern tube has severed the keel completely with drastic results. It can amount to breaking the craft's back. For some reason such points are often forgotten, owners shrug their shoulders and say 'Oh it'll be all right,' but very often it is not and it is craft such as this that have led to the question mark being placed behind the word conversion. It can also account for the extremely low price of some boats. But such a craft can never be cheap at any price since their value as a seagoing craft is nothing at all. They are fit only for scrap.

Before knocking conversions any further let's look at a few comparisons in a little more detail. Since I have already mentioned the ship's lifeboat I will begin with that.

**Ship's
Lifeboat**

Most often the ship's lifeboat is a double ender with a high stern. Fig. 88. The idea of a high pointed stern is to help the low powered craft to ride to a high sea without being pooped or having the sea come aboard from astern. They are also less likely to broach. With the comparatively fine waterline section the ship's lifeboat moves easily under the power of oars only. This allows the craft to be pulled clear of burning or distressed ships. They are usually built with sealed buoyancy tanks to keep the craft afloat even when waterlogged and fitted with emergency equipment to look after the souls onboard.

Happily most lifeboats are never used in an emergency and spend their lives slung high in the davits of the mothership, touching the water only for the periodic inspection and test. Most of the older lifeboats were of clinker or double diagonal construction and, as anyone who has owned a clinker boat will know, it will deteriorate far more quickly out of the water than in it. Out of the water the timber dries in the sun and air, often causing planks to split and timbers to crack. It is a case of damage caused by lack of use rather than overwork.

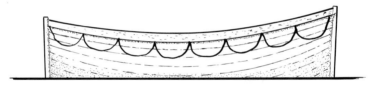

Fig 88. Ship's lifeboat.

Just in passing, a simple test to check if this type of wooden boat is cranky is to stand to the side at one end and to give the boat a good shaking. If it wobbles like a jelly it is cranky and best left alone, if on the other hand, the boat stays firm under your onslaught that is a good sign.

Many make their first mistake when they try to disguise the lifeboat. Often it is the sheerline that is altered first in an attempt to make the stern look less high. This seldom works since it does not run in the same sweet lines of the planking. It does, in fact, look distinctly odd. The next common mistake is to stick a cabin on it; very often just a large box is plonked onto the top; with square holes cut out for windows, the craft becomes more and more repulsive. Add to this handrails that are made from galvanized water pipe, complete with fittings, and a paint job that makes the added part stand out from the original and the result is a boat that looks precisely what it is, a botch-up. My illustration Fig. 89 is not an exaggeration, such craft always remind me of a circus clown's car that is going to fall to bits at any moment.

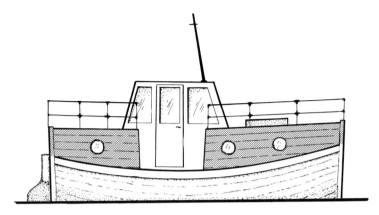

Fig 89. Lifeboat with a cabin plonked on the top.

The sad thing is, that with the right approach, most of these boats could be made into very respectable conversions. In fact my sketch Fig. 90, is a lovely conversion I know very well; it has made some excellent passages and, probably more important, looks every bit the little ship she is. This is a good example of a satisfying and successful conversion; yet it is the same basic lifeboat as used in Fig. 89 and the pity is that they both could be listed under the same heading. For the first time buyer with limited resources Fig. 90 could be an ideal boat on which to cut his teeth.

Fig 90. A good lifeboat conversion.

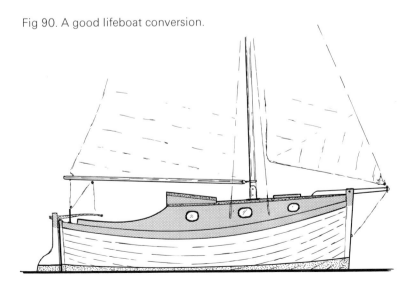

One of my earliest memories of boats features a craft called 'Grey Fox'. As a young boy I knew little of the technicalities of conversions and I did not even know the owners, but I remember clearly the river gossip of her travels, and she was probably one of the simplest yet most effective conversions I have ever seen. Retired from the R.N.L.I. service, this very special type of lifeboat made a superb cruising yacht. The builder or owner, I still do not know who, retained the sweeping sheer and double ended features with all the character that goes with it, adding only the smallest coach-roof. Fig. 91.

Instead of attempting expensive structural alterations to disguise the craft's noble origins the emphasis was put on transforming her from a workhorse into a yacht. The topsides glittered reflections in her beautiful finish; her spars and new coach-roof gleamed under the many coats of varnish. She was as proud as any little ship and the feature of her part of the river. It seems a shame to call craft like this a conversion at all because they are certainly worthy of more consideration.

Fig 91. An excellent R.N.L.I. lifeboat conversion.

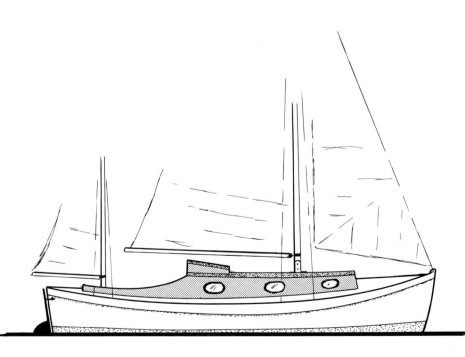

Speed   The newcomer to boats is often disillusioned by the craft's performance. Strangely they often tend to relate the speed of a boat with that of a motor car and ultimately are disappointed to discover the enormous difference. A little very basic knowledge on this subject would prepare the would-be boat owner and save him that disillusionment.

Full displacement type boats, yachts, lifeboats, heavy fishing boats and the like, are designed to pass through the water rather than over it like a speedboat. The effective design speed of a displacement hull is determined by its waterline length rather than the power of its engines. This design speed is related to the wave it creates as the hull passes through the water. Maximum design speed is reached when the length of the wave is the same as the waterline length of the craft. Fig. 92A.

Attempts to make the boat go faster are common and often futile. What in effect happens is that when the boat is pushed faster the bow-wave increases with the result that the boat tries to climb over its own bow-wave but cannot. This causes a heavy wake, a waste of fuel and power but very little increase in speed. Fig. 92B.

Fig 92. Maximum speed of a displacement hull is reached when the length of the wave she makes equals her waterline length (A). Attempts to go faster (B) only create a bigger wave.

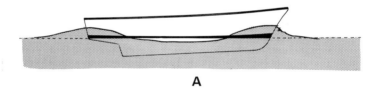

A

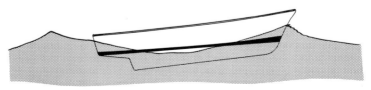

B

To illustrate this I watched a man convert a lifeboat with a design speed of $7\frac{1}{2}$ knots. It was calculated that a single 40 horsepower engine would give him $6\frac{1}{2}$ knots; the man fitted TWO 40 horsepower motors and the resulting speed was 8 knots. Thus an extra engine, with its propeller, shaft, tank and all the ancillary bits actually gave him only $1\frac{1}{2}$ knots of extra speed, an application of brute force to yield very little indeed for so much expense.

In Table 6, I have listed the approximate design speeds for a selection of hull lengths, but it is important to note that the figures are approximate, and relate only to hulls of full displacement configuration. Do not use the chart for boats of hard chine configuration as these often fall into the planing or semi-displacement category with quite different performances.

Table 6. Approximate design speed of displacement boats of varying waterline length.

Waterline length in feet	Speed in knots
18	5
24	$6\frac{3}{4}$
26	7
30	$7\frac{1}{2}$
35	$8\frac{1}{4}$
40	9

From a structural point of view conversions are often complex and must be something of a compromise, mainly because the craft, before conversion, was a working boat designed for lifesaving, fishing or military purposes. For instance in the R.N.L.I. lifeboat, all emphasis is on safety, with little thought given to accommodation, save for shelter. Many complete bulkheads subdivide the craft into watertight compartments, making it difficult to fit in living accommodation when it comes to be transformed into a yacht. The compromise entails knowing how much to remove while still retaining enough structural strength. Remove the wrong walls of a house and the whole thing could come falling down, but with a boat such a collapse would probably wait until she was caught out in a storm.

Another point to remember is that the wiring and plumbing in a work boat usually runs on the surface as for the seaman it is better that it is on show; yet the elegance of a yacht requires these things routed out of sight. It is quite impractical to think of stripping these things out to have them refitted in a less conspicuous place so it is one of those things one just has to live with.

Everything on lifeboats seems to be built to excess. Even a simple light switch is a large bulky fitting that will work underwater and switches the light on and off with a resounding clonk. But it all works and goes on working long after normal fittings have failed.

Ballast and keels are other things that lifeboat conversions seem to be fitted with in a variety of ways, some of them unorthodox. Bilges flooded with concrete are fairly common. In some cases the concrete is encapsulating pig-iron or other weights. I came across one with pieces of old iron, bedsteads, even the tip of an old engine block sticking out through the concrete like the bones of an old ship dying in the mud.

Others have an external iron ballast keel. I have seen resourceful owners utilize a length of railway track for this purpose.

Two points to be wary of with external ballast:

(i) How is it all fixed to the hull? Through-bolts must be used and provision should be made to distribute the loading on the inside of the keel.

(ii) The normal type of lifeboat can be beached taking only a slight heel. Fig. 93A. The addition of an external keel would mean that in the same situation the boat would heel over much further. Fig. 93B. So the use of sea-legs would normally be considered.

Fig. 93. Extending the keel means that the boat will heel more when aground.

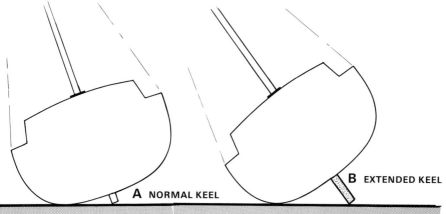

A NORMAL KEEL

B EXTENDED KEEL

Some ships' lifeboats are fitted with centreboards and others may have them fitted during conversion. As with the stern tube there is a real danger of severely weakening the craft's back if an attempt is made to cut it through the centre keel. A better idea is to reinforce the garboard strake and fit the centreboard there, as it will make little difference if slightly off centre.

Many lifeboats show signs of their conditions and age by many repairs. Patches and short-ends of planking are common; inside, the doubling-up of timbers and generous coats of tar or other bituminous paints do tend to reflect that a hull is tired and even cranky or rotten. Heroic stories of the boat's past must not blind you to the fact that you are interested in the future.

Racing Yachts Conversions are not restricted to lifeboats and military craft, there are a great many others. Racing yachts are sometimes converted for cruising. A great many sleek thoroughbred racing yachts have been transformed into cruising boats with a whole variety of results. Fig. 94.

(A) A typical boat as it would have been originally; a racing craft pure and simple with little or no accommodation at all.

(B) An attractive conversion that retains much of the original charm; it looks well done and is not obviously a conversion. This boat is unlikely to have full standing headroom since this style of racing craft is very fine in the bilge.

(C) Another conversion on the same hull, but this time the owner has gone for full standing headroom and given the outward appearance very little thought indeed. It is a strange fact that people building and converting become so much in love with the boat that they cannot see any wrong, so it is true that beauty is in the eye of the beholder. Another point to notice is that the original rig would need to be reduced to clear the new superstructure, which will naturally affect the performance.

A pure racing boat would not be fitted with an engine and as mentioned for ships' lifeboats the keel may not be wide enough to accept the sterngear without causing severe weakness. It is fairly common to see the engine fitted on the wing, that is to one side, or even with the engine on the centreline and its shaft and tube going out to one side of the keel; the shaft would then be supported by an 'A' bracket. Sometimes a self feathering propeller is fitted to reduce drag.

Pre-war boats of this type were often fitted with external lead keels and I have seen several that have lost these, presumably for the high price of scrap, and an iron keel substituted when internal ballast may be added to make up the difference in weight.

Fig 94. Racing yachts converted for cruising.

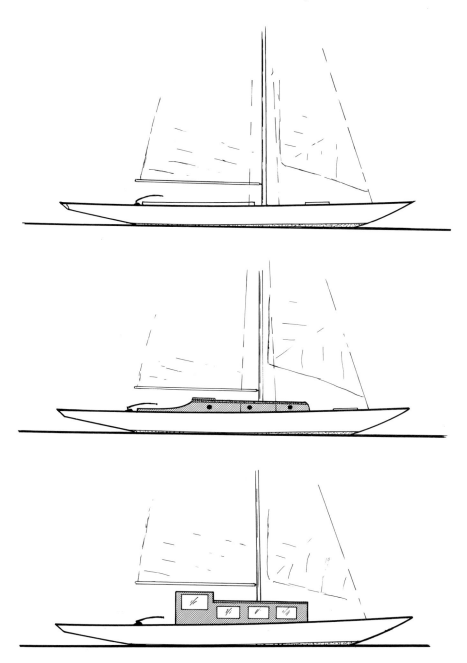

Work Boats   Some of the most natural craft to find a new life as yachts are the
many traditional work boats from around the British coastline. There are
dozens of different types, each one being developed over the
generations to suit the many and various jobs required of them. To
mention but three, Falmouth Quay Punt, the Brixham Trawler and the
Itchen Ferry Boat, all are to be found now operating as yachts. Fig. 95,
the Itchen Ferry Boat is still being produced in its native Solent area
but now updated as a yacht and produced in G.R.P.

This type of boat can very often be changed into a yacht with very
little, if any, alteration from the original. Sometimes the large hold
space below is transformed into accommodation without the addition
of a coachroof or deckhouse. This type of craft can often be picked-up
very cheaply although extreme care should be taken because the cost
of any major repairs to such craft would be very expensive indeed. So
roomy are many of this type of traditional boat that they very often
become a complete home.

The spars of this type of boat were mainly solid pine with sails of
canvas. Straight stems and bowsprits were characteristic features of
most. Many had surprisingly fine lines and a good turn of speed. A long
straight keel is another feature common to most of them.

Fig 95. Itchen ferry boat.

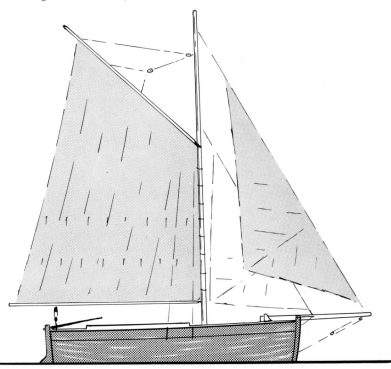

Motor Fishing Vessels

The M.F.V. (motor fishing vessel) is another very popular craft for conversion which can often be transformed into a yacht very easily. This type of craft is very heavily constructed in a great range of sizes from about 30 feet upwards, although the most commonly found sizes are in the 40 to 50 feet range. It is worth noting that although called a motor FISHING vessel many hundreds were built for a whole range of other duties. Fig. 96 shows such a craft now in use as a yacht without any external alterations at all, save for the paint job. Other M.F.V.'s I have seen have had fortunes spent on them; starting with a complete gutting-out job and then complete rebuilding to the owners' requirements, followed by the installation of central heating and deepfreeze.

The full rounded section of the M.F.V. is carvel planked with that high unmistakable stem. Most commonly they were single screw with a low revving thumper diesel engine and large propeller. Some were fitted with steadying sails and I have even seen them fitted with extremely expensive stabilizers. This type of craft could be made into a floating home with a world wide cruising potential.

Converting a secondhand hull is one way to get a reasonable boat with the minimum of cost. The results can be pleasing and give many happy hours both in the conversion itself and the sailing. But to be right it has to look right and that requires an experienced eye; it in doubt, there are plenty of craftsmen around our boatyards who would be glad to give advice, all you need do is ask.

Fig 96. Motor fishing vessel.

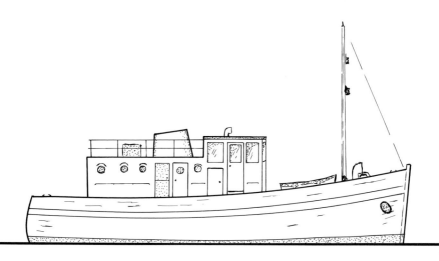

Hardwoods

Wood	Average weight cu. ft.	Resistance	Qualities	Use
AGBA	31	Resistant	Nails, glues and screws well. Works easily. Stable.	Small craft planking, decking. Hot moulding.
AFROMOSIA	44	Very resistant	Has tendency to split. Easy to work. Glues well. Very stable.	Keel, stem, floors, frames, beams.
ASH	44	Not resistant	Works easily. Fixes well. May distort.	Timbers, tillers, boathooks, cleats.
CEDAR	30	Resistant	Very easy to work. Glues and screws well. Stable.	Planking on light weight craft.
ROCK ELM	48	Moderately resistant	Hard. Glues, screws and nails well.	Bent timbers, rudders.
WYCH ELM	38	Not resistant	Fairly easy to work. Not stable.	Rubbing strakes. Belting.
IROKO	40	Very resistant	Hard. Screws, nails and glues well. May distort.	Beam shelf, floors, decking, grown frames.
MAHOGANY, AFRICAN	38	Moderately resistant	Good general purpose timber. Stable.	Planking, decking.
MAHOGANY, HONDURAS	34	Resistant	High quality timber. Good to work. Stable.	Joinery work. Planking.
MAKORE	39	Resistant	Works well. Fixes and glues well. Stable.	Keel, stems, deadwood floors.
OBECHE	24	Not resistant	Easy to work. Fixes and glues well. Not too stable.	Interior joinery work.
OAK	45	Resistant	Hard to work. Fixes and glues well. Not too stable.	Keel, stem, deadwood floors, grown frames.
SAPELE	39	Moderately resistant	Good to work. Nails, screws and glues well. Not too stable.	Planking, keels, stem, covering board, King planks.

				Almost everything.
		...ce to work. Tendency to split. Precautions needed for gluing. Very stable.		
UTILE	41	Resistant	Nice to work. Screws and glues well.	Planking, joinery.

APPENDIX II

Softwoods

Wood	Average weight cu. ft.	Resistance	Qualities	Use
CEDAR WESTERN RED	24	Resistant	Easy to work. Glues and screws well. Stable	Decking, lightweight planking.
DOUGLAS FIR	33	Moderately resistant	Easy to work. Glues and screws well. Very resinous. Fairly stable.	Decking, beam shelfs, stringer. Solid spars.
HEWLOCK	30	Not resistant	Easy to work. Glues and screws well. Fairly stable.	General joinery work.
LARCH	35	Resistant	Easy to work. Glues and fixes well. Fairly stable.	Planking, chines, stringer, decking.
PARANA PINE	34	Not resistant	Easy to work. Tends to split. Not too stable.	Not an ideal boat-building material.
PITCH PINE	42	Very resistant	Nice to work. Resinous. Stable.	Planking, decking, beams, stringers.
REDWOOD	32	Moderately resistant	Easy to work. Glues and screws well. Stable.	Planking, decking and stringers.
SITKA SPRUCE	28	Not resistant	Easy to work. Glues and fixes well. Stable.	Oars, spars, decking, beams, planking.

Index